Tattoos of the Heart

For Bill —
All the best!

Dianne
Schwab

Tattoos of the Heart

◆

A Matter of Life and Death and Points of Interest In-between

Dianne Schread

Writer's Showcase
New York Lincoln Shanghai

Tattoos of the Heart
A Matter of Life and Death and Points of Interest In-between

All Rights Reserved © 1998, 2003 by Dianne Schread

No part of this book may be reproduced or transmitted in any form or by any means, graphic, electronic, or mechanical, including photocopying, recording, taping, or by any information storage retrieval system, without the written permission of the publisher.

Writer's Showcase
an imprint of iUniverse, Inc.

For information address:
iUniverse, Inc.
2021 Pine Lake Road, Suite 100
Lincoln, NE 68512
www.iuniverse.com

ISBN: 0-595-26703-3 (pbk)
ISBN: 0-595-74562-8 (cloth)

Printed in the United States of America

Dedicated to my sons:
Mark, Paul, Stephen and Cayce

A special word of thanks

I could never have finished this book without the encouragement of my family and friends. I am indebted to my devoted husband, Jerry, who entertained himself for hours while I worked on this manuscript and my loyal ballroom dancing friends: Pat and David Ingram, Norma and Bob Planner, and Mae and Dick Olson, who continually encourage and lift me up when I falter. I am especially grateful to my best friend, Pat, who has encouraged and supported me in every endeavor and who constantly cheers me on to my goal.

*Written in awe of God's redeeming power
and as a testimony to God's work in my life*

Contents

Preface xv
Tattoos of the Heart 1
- ***In God's time*** 3
- ***Stillborn*** 4

In the beginning 5
- ***My Prayer*** 8

From a child's perspective 9
Realistic optimism 15
- *Expectations* 17
- *God's Exceeding Great Joy!* 18

Depression 19
School days 21
- *Can you hear?* 22

Puppy love, loss and guilt 23
- *Fun=Happiness? No!* 28

For all the wrong reasons 29
- *Stepping out in faith* 32

Recipe for despair 33
Moving toward divorce 39
Trouble in Paradise 43

Heading in the wrong direction 47
A matter of life or death 55
- *Forgiveness* 60

I can't believe he took the kids 61
Going home 65
How could I have done that? 69
- **Noel, Noel, Noel** 75
- **Missing You** 76

My baby comes home 77
- **We, Lovers, Friends** 80

Rejected! 81
- *Rejection* 82
- *The final rejection* 83
- *On being content* 84

In the depths of despair, I sank even lower 85
- *Life is too short* 88

This time, the light at the end of the tunnel was not
an oncoming train! 89
Life begins at "forty" 93
- *Attitude adjustment* 96

The ultimatum 97
Trying to make some sense of it 99
Right on my doorstep 103
- *Diversion* 110

Back to work 111
Starting a new life 115

On a downhill slide. 121

Is anyone there? 129
- ***Thoughts of love***. 137
- ***A note to the one I love***. 138
- ***Don't forget the little things***. 139
- ***Julie*** 140

The Lord giveth and the Lord taketh away!. 141
- ***If my daddy could have spoken*** 143
- ***Master Plan***. 145

A wedding, a funeral and more 147
- *Life isn't always fair* 149
- *Endurance*. 150
- *Invalidation*. 151
- *Color-blind* 152

An open letter to my sons. 153
- ***If one good thing leads to another, it's okay to feel good about yourself!*** 159
- *Think twice!*. 160

The healing continues. 161
- *Past vs. present* 165
- *Burdens* 166

The challenge of a lifetime 167
- ***Mother, the sweetest one*** 171
- *Laugh* 172

If only we could see the end from the beginning. 173
- ***A time to grow up***. 176

It's coming to an end. Or, is this just the beginning?. 177

- *God's pathway* 180
- God blessed me with furry friends 181
  - *Surprises* 184
- In closing 185
  - ***A sinner's prayer*** 187
- 2003 update 189
- Author's note 191
- Letters from Mark, a.k.a. David, the Poet, Paul, Stephen and Cayce 193
  - *Leave!* 200
- Statistics 201

Note: Listings for Nuggets of Insight are in italics.
Original poems are in bold italics.

Preface

Nothing is quite as painfully permanent as a tattoo! The pain of the needle is only the beginning. Later, the pain of healing begins. After healing, for those of us who have regrets, the pain of wearing a brand is still there for all to see.

I discovered that to remove the tattoo would not only be expensive. It would be physically and emotionally painful as well. Even the removal process left a scar that I have to explain. If I explain the scar, I have to explain the tattoo. The stages of recovery are similar to the healing process one goes through in counseling and therapy to deal with the emotional "tattoos" of life.

A thirty-minute adventure in a tattoo parlor left a permanent mark on my wrist and my psyche. I would like to plead impetuous youth. If I said that my sixteen-year-old son, Mark, was with me and tried to discourage me, then, that would be the painful truth.

Most of us can point to many events in our lives that have indelibly engraved themselves upon our hearts. These marks are emotional tattoos on our hearts.

You may have seen a tattooed person at the circus or on "Ripley's Believe it or Not." You probably wondered why they had subjected themselves to the pain. As you read this book, you will wonder how anyone could wander through life collecting such painful emotional tattoos, without seeming to learn from them.

My story may read like bad fiction, yet, it is undeniably true. Although it took many years, I finally woke up. With God's help, I made the necessary changes and moved forward with confidence. It is my hope that my story will inspire someone to wake up and take charge of their life before they sink to the depths as I did.

I realize that I have traveled a most incredible journey. I would never have believed I could have gotten here from there, but I have!

In an essay entitled *The Station* by Robert J. Hastings, he tells us that the stations we constantly seek to attain in this life are mere illusions. The journey is the joy. For much of my life I wasted my energy looking for the station. Consequently, my journey was anything but joyful.

Much later, I came to realize that, when I remembered to focus on the journey instead of circumstances, the peace of God that "passeth understanding" would see me through.

Yes. I did get here from there, and if I can do it, perhaps you can find your way as well.

Preface

A support group counselor writes:

Dianne,

I just finished reading your book. I was unable to put it down and read it almost in one sitting. This is your story and you tell it well. The reader is there with you all the way. I experienced pain and sadness, was touched by your "From a Child's Perspective" and often I wanted to tell you "NO, NO, Don't DO THAT." It is truly amazing how you have survived.

However, I felt a sense of hope as I read the final pages of the book. I believe that writing this book was very therapeutic for you. It is an excellent example of journaling. Your story will encourage others and they can envision a hope and a future for themselves.

I believe there are many people who have just about lost all hope. It is my prayer that through reading your book they may turn to God and His Word to seek forgiveness, peace, hope and a new beginning. God is so good to us. He loves us and doesn't give up on us, even if we give up on ourselves.

Finally, I would like to leave one of my favorite scriptures with you: Jeremiah 29:11 (NIV) "For I know the plans I have for you, declares the Lord, plans to prosper you and not to harm you, plans to give you hope and a future." Isn't that a wonderful promise?

Best wishes,

Barbara

P.S. Your poems are wonderful!

Tattoos of the Heart

In God's time

Perhaps we'd have met much sooner than this,
This wonderful man and me.
But I went my own way and rejected God's will
For too many years, you see.

From opposite lifestyles each of us came,
With different philosophies we played at life's game.
He with his social life in a whirl;
I, as a lonely little girl.

Both of us looking for love it seems,
But finding it only in our dreams.
We had lived out our lives and suffered alone,
And when I came to my senses…my youth was gone!

After trying life's worst and sampling its best,
I felt I had finally passed God's test.
Then one day it happened…God sent him to me.
And, we couldn't be happier now, you see.

I'm just where I should have been, right from the start.
If only I'd waited…and let God do His part.

Stillborn

Today the world is black
Nature shivers from the cold,
Windy drafts blow down her back
Sharp as swords stuck in her soul.

Hovering near are angels weeping
Grieving for the woman sleeping.
No cry will usher in this morn.
Today a child missed being born.

Nancy Newbold Cochran
used with permission

In the beginning

My father was in his late twenties, my mother nine years younger, when they met. After a very short engagement, they were married. They obviously were right for each other. They were opposites. My father was physically strong, yet depended heavily on my mother emotionally. My mother was physically weak, yet emotionally strong, though high strung as my father put it.

Their first child was premature and stillborn and they were inconsolable. In spite of the doctor's warnings against another pregnancy, sixteen months later I was born. They wanted me so much that they were willing to risk everything to have me. I felt loved and a sense of security surrounded me. On the negative side, however, that kind of love demands an uncompromising loyalty. I found these demands impossible to meet. It ultimately seemed as though my parents expected me to give up my own identity and become a replica of them.

You may have heard it said, "You are what you eat." That may very well be true, but the essence of your self is much more complex than that. So much so, that many never truly realize exactly who they are!

We all know that an expectant mother who drinks or does drugs may do irreversible damage to her baby. Many deliver neurologically damaged babies with Fetal Alcohol Syndrome or crack-addicted infants, who then live out their lives in misery and pain. We also know that a nursing infant takes into its body the drugs that the mother is taking.

We know that stress is playing a key role in the lack of good health. Sure, you may not feel sick. Although you have no major illness, can you say that you really feel well? Are you relaxed and content?

Do you remember the physical and emotional sensations of fight or flight? Have they been with you so constantly that you no longer distinguish them as defense mechanisms but consider them just a part of your life? A saying that I heard a few years ago has become my motto: If you don't want to fight and you can't flee, FLOW! Too bad that philosophy came to me so late in life.

While my mother carried me in her womb, she was still grieving over the loss of her first daughter, a stillborn. The doctor thought it would be best for Mother if she didn't see or touch the baby. For my mother, this baby existed only in her dreams.

I can't even begin to imagine the pain of that loss. It must have devastated her. The fact that her baby was premature made it appear that my mother could have been pregnant before her marriage. It was an era when society ostracized a woman for such a sin. She experienced an irrational sense of guilt. Coupled with her loss and grief, it led to a spiraling depression.

This was the toxic stuff surrounding my conception. This emotional tidal wave assaulted the womb that nurtured me as a developing fetus. It is small wonder, considering today's medical findings that I was in physical and possibly mental distress at birth. This distress exhibited itself as unrelenting crying for the first nine months of my life. Surely, this must have affected my psyche. In retrospect, I believe this was probably the first of my heart's tattoos.

It was an especially difficult time for my mother because she wanted a baby, but not one that was always crying. She told me that she had prayed to die, or for us both to die. She was so desperate that she would have chosen almost any avenue of escape. My mother felt powerless to fix whatever was wrong with me.

She held the common belief of the early forties that babies and small children didn't understand what was going on. She spoke those prayers aloud in my presence. My mother had no idea that as a nursing infant in her arms I would feel and absorb some of her despair.

My Prayer

Lord, give me eyes Thy beauty to see.
And give me a voice to speak for Thee.
Lord, give me an ear to hear Thy call.
And, Lord give me strength lest I should fall.
Oh, Lord use my hands to do Thy will.
And guide my feet in Thy way still.
And plant in my heart Thy Word for me,
That it will burst forth for all to see.
Lord, heal my heart and help me make
Tomorrow a brand-new start.

From a child's perspective

Note: I believe that we accept our own perception as reality. I wrote this essay based on what I believe was my infantile perception. When I was eighteen months old, I had scarlet fever and diphtheria. I spent nineteen days in a hospital isolation ward. I didn't see my parents until it was time to go home. For years, I listened to stories about that time and how I behaved when I came home. To heal the child within me, I imagined myself as that innocent baby and the emotional pain she must have felt.

Here I am. I was due to arrive in July, but my mother's doctor who induced her labor with a dose of castor oil assigned my June birthday to me. Am I ready to come into the world? Maybe I am. Maybe not. Am I angry? Probably, however, at this age, I cannot yet distinguish between emotions. No one has stacked them neatly and labeled them for me.

I do feel something; however, it is *not* pleasant. It is something so overwhelming that I cry out in pain. I have cried so often and for such a long time that my mother suspects colic (whatever that is). This time of pain has now lasted for about nine months. I have become so frustrated and confused by this discomfort and lack of rest that I feel like a zombie. I am trying so very hard not to acknowledge my feelings anymore.

Things are becoming better; the pain has gone, but not the memory of it or my mother holding me and rocking me for hours trying to comfort me. I smile a lot, I gurgle and amuse myself and convince everyone that I am normal (whatever that is).

Tattoos of the Heart

I am getting bigger, but I don't have any hair! Everyone is worried that I am going to be bald like my grandfather. I like my grandfather. He is so pleasant. He has a black change purse that he carries in his pocket. In addition, he wears BIG boots! I like the boot game he plays with me. He takes his boots and clumps them along on the floor as if to chase me while I squeal and run away.

Granddaddy taught me to close my eyes and hold out my hand every time he takes out the little black purse. Then he places some coins in my hands for me to feed my clown bank. My grandmother is afraid that he is spoiling me.

The clown bank is so funny. You put the coin on the clown's tongue and push his belly button and he swallows the money! The clown is always smiling. I think he likes the taste of the coin. I don't! I tried it once!

My grandmother loves to hold me and rock me in her big rocking chair. While she is holding me, she is absentmindedly half-scratching, half-tickling my back. I could sit and enjoy that for hours. It makes me relax and get so sleepy that I can barely stay awake. I think that she is spoiling me, and I love it!

I woke up this morning earlier than usual and I was very hot and felt so sick. Why do I feel this way? What is happening to me? Where are they taking me? Why are my mother and daddy crying?

Why is my mother giving me to these people? Where are we going? Where is my dolly? I never go anywhere without my dolly. I can't go to sleep without her!

The room they have left me in is so ugly! My room at home has pink curtains and nursery characters on the linoleum floor.

From a child's perspective

Where is my mother? Why don't these strange people sing to me or rock me? My mother always rocks me and sings to me when I am sick. It makes me feel safe.

Why don't these people talk to me? Why are their clothes white instead of pretty, bright colors? I don't like their white dresses. My mother has pretty dresses with flowers on them.

Why are they hurting me again? They whisper among themselves words like scarlet fever, diphtheria, contagious, serious, and not much hope. What does it mean? I don't understand. They are just words. I can't talk. I can't even say the word mother. Buh is my word for mother. How can they expect me to understand the language of these doctors and nurses?

Where is my daddy? Why doesn't he come and read the funnies to me? He used to carry me around the room and tell me about the pictures on the wall. No pictures are on these walls. I miss my daddy!

Why don't they talk to me? My daddy always talks to me. Why don't they rock me in the big rocking chair? Who will tell me a story? My daddy knows many stories.

Why don't they tell me they love me? Buh tells me she loves me every time she holds me. Where is she? Buh? Buh! I hardly have the strength to cry or call for her. Why doesn't she answer?

She doesn't care! If she did, she would be here! I did *not* leave her. She brought me here and left me!

I can't even remember what my daddy looks like. I always looked at Buh's face while she nursed me. I will always remember the way she looked.

I don't understand what is happening to me. I am only eighteen months old and have been here in the hospital for many days. It seems as if I have always been here. As I lie here in the isolation ward with nothing to do but think, my memories of things become confused and blurred.

I try to remember my mother and the thing I remember best is the way she sang to me as she rocked me. My mother seemed to feel better when she sang. She always smiled. She usually sang hymns to me, but sometimes she sang funny songs, too.

Oh! No! Here they are with the scissors again. No! I can't scream; I am too weak. No! Silently I plead, Please don't do it again, but they do. The scissors are so big and they swish as they cut the tape. They always cut the tape first so it will be ready. It hurts when they jerk away the old tape so they can remove my diaper. Then they tape another one to me.

Did they lose the pins? Buh has pins. Why don't they get them from her? Won't she give the pins to these people?

Why do they hurt me so? Maybe, if I try very hard, I can stop soiling my diaper and they will not do these things again!

Buh? Buh! I want to go home. I want a cookie. Buh? Do you remember me? Where are you?

Ouch! The nurse stuck me again with that awful needle. She says I look like a pincushion (whatever that is). If pincushions feel like this, I definitely don't want to be one!

I am beginning to get so sleepy. I can hardly keep my eyes open. I thought I heard my daddy talking to me, but I can barely focus my eyes. I must be dreaming. I sense someone lying on the bed next to me. I think it must be my daddy. The doctor is telling him what he is going to do as he prepares to administer a direct blood transfusion from my daddy to me.

From a child's perspective

I don't know what is going on. I don't know about transfusions. Just as I drift off, I see the tubes attached to my leg become red with the very essence of life from my daddy's veins. I feel so peaceful now, so secure for the first time since I got here!

The next day I could barely open my eyes. I was still so sleepy, but I smelled something good. It smelled like breakfast!

Suddenly, I am hungry for the first time in days! I can hardly wait. I feel good. I am not so hot now. I can't remember when I felt so cool.

I don't believe it! The doctors and nurses are smiling at me! They must be happy today. That makes me happy. I was so tired of seeing such long faces. I feel like smiling today, too. I remember my dream about my daddy. Was it real? What were they doing in my dream? What was that red stuff in the tubes?

Uh oh, I must have fallen asleep. What are they saying? I hear the doctors and nurses whispering in the hall. I hear words like survive. What does that mean? Is it good or bad? I heard the doctor say, "She is going to survive." Does that mean I am worse? Oh dear, what is to become of me?

Buh! Where are you?

It feels so good to get that IV needle out of my leg. I wonder what is going on. The nurse just smiled at me. She says we are going to take a trip! Oh, will I ever get to see my mother and daddy again?

They are taking me somewhere. I am so scared. I don't know where we are going. I don't remember this hallway or the stairs.

Then, I see them! Buh! Buh!

Buhhhh. That is all I can say. Is that really you? Who is that man with you? His face looks so thin and drawn. Is that my daddy?

Tattoos of the Heart

Buh? Buh is my refuge, a protective covering, a heartbeat that matches my own as I lay against her breast.

Buh, Please don't ever leave me again!

Realistic optimism

My cup always seems half-full. That is the way I see life. Perhaps this is why I never completely gave in to fear. Moreover, along with being an optimist, I am a realist. Consequently, I can see that the half-full cup is also a dirty dish to wash! I am glad to call myself a realistic optimist.

It is my opinion that all people come into this world as potential optimists. However, in infancy or childhood, it seems that many learn to be pessimists. Fortunately, even the dramatic circumstances that were so traumatic to me only served to kindle my optimism. That optimism and my faith in God helped me to survive the many bouts of depression that I have faced over the years.

I grew up in a slower-paced society than one born after 1960 might fully appreciate. We had time for daydreaming, planning, and imagination.

As a young child, radio was the medium of entertainment and it required one to exercise their imagination. When I was nine years old, television came into our lives and we watched it right through the national anthem at night.

In the early days, television provided real entertainment and often positively reinforced moral values. Television programming was idealistic and presented life in an upbeat, dignified way, with basic moral standards portrayed as the norm.

Then the soaps moved to TV. Although I had listened to soap operas on the radio during the summer, they didn't seem as real as they did on television. One could quickly become addicted to their favorite shows and vicariously experience things they would never dare to do in real life. I think the story lines may not have influenced older, mature adults as much as the younger generation. After all, their morals came from a generation that was not so permissive. However, for me, it was an insidious assault against the training and teachings that my parents had sought to instill in me.

In retrospect, I realize that if one embraces something close enough and long enough it seems to become, if not okay, at least acceptable or tolerable. I believe the mixed messages I was receiving contributed to my emotional downfall and the disgraceful lifestyle I adopted. Unfortunately, I surrendered control of my life and its direction for many years. Then, when I tried to put my life back together, it took several more years for things to fall into place.

Although I always had an underlying deep and abiding faith, I lacked the commitment and inner strength to live it. Thank God, however, I never completely gave up hope! Eventually, I began to turn my life around by giving up control and allowing God to work in me. As I matured, I changed tremendously. As I charted a new course, I discovered that I really wanted to know how and why I had gone so far astray. I dug deeply into my past and my present, to discover why I had permitted these things to happen to me.

As I embarked on my journey through the painful years of my past, I contemplated the question: WHO am I? Even as I began, I wasn't completely sure I wanted all the answers. I revisited each stop along the way and I gained valuable insight as I began to accept the person I had been. Gradually I could relate my past to my present. I could then see that this journey had already begun to change the course of my future.

Expectations

I often pause to consider and wonder why others think that I would be happier if confined within the small box of their expectations, which contains who they mistakenly think I am.

David, the Poet
used with permission

God's Exceeding Great Joy!

God doesn't love the prodigal more. However, as the Gentle Shepherd, He rejoices with "exceeding great joy" when one of His lambs returns to the safety of the fold!

Depression

Depression has been a frequent companion for as long as I can consciously remember. I was four years old when I had the first episode. I had always wanted a sibling, perhaps to take the spotlight off me, since I wasn't the answer to my parent's dreams. As a small child, I begged my parents for a baby sister. Although my mother's doctor advised against it, my parents tried in vain to have another child. I have no idea how different my life would have been if they had succeeded, but I am sure it would have had quite an impact.

When I was four years old, they placed me in a nursery school so that I would have other children to play with. The short time I spent in the school was memorable. Mats were on the floor for afternoon naps and I experienced a taste I will never forget: graham crackers with a vanilla pudding sauce.

The first day, when I came home, I told my parents I knew how to tell boy babies from girl babies. This disturbed them immensely. The second day, I told them I went to the potty with other children in the room. This did *not* set well with my mother. She was extremely modest and she had trained me to be modest as well. Because of the things I told them about the nursery, my parents withdrew me immediately.

As it turned out, I really didn't know the difference between boy and girl babies. When my parents questioned me about the subject, I said, "Oh, that's easy, they cry differently!" As a normal four-year-old, I was curious about everything, but especially the subject that had caused so much commotion. My parents dealt with my curiosity by shaming me to the point that I no longer wanted to live.

The shame I felt was so emotionally devastating that the pain seemed almost physical. In a fit of anger and subsequent depression, I wished aloud that I were dead. My mother immediately told me that God was listening and was very disappointed with me. She said God might punish me by striking me dead if I continued to say such terrible things. In my four-year-old mentality, I envisioned this as the ultimate escape. From that point on, I frequently wished to die!

When my frequent attempts to provoke God into striking me dead failed, punishing myself became a way of life for me. I gravitated to abusive partners and had relationships with them that perpetuated the punishment I thought I deserved.

One Sunday, when I was five, we were on the bus headed to visit my daddy's parents. All of the seats were taken and we had to stand. A soldier offered to hold me and they let me sit with him. Before the ride was over, I was engaged to him. I forget whose idea it was, but the whole thing really embarrassed my mother. My mother often reminded me of the incident over the years as I went through one marriage after another. That childish incident seemed to have been prophetic concerning the direction my life would take when I grew up.

For my fifth birthday, I received a beautiful gold bracelet with my name engraved on it. I still have that bracelet. It is the only memento left from my childhood. Receiving such a wonderful present confused me. Then it made me angry and depressed. If I were such a bad child, why did I get a present? In my emotional distress, I rubbed the face of the bracelet on the steps and wore away part of the gold. However, it did *not* erase my name. Many years later, through therapy, I came to understand that I was literally trying to erase myself by making myself nameless!

School days

At the age of six, with wide-eyed wonder and Shirley Temple curls, I said "good-bye" to my mother and entered my first grade classroom. More children were in that one room than I even knew existed! My only peer group experiences were in a small class in Sunday School. I was glad to see that a few of my friends from that group were in my class.

Learning was such fun and easy too, but the playground was tough! For six years, I had played mostly by myself. Now I needed to learn how to play with other children. I also needed to learn how to get them to include me in their play. I couldn't seem to figure out what I needed to do to be popular and I suffered a perpetual loneliness that I did *not* understand. It was so painful at times that I immersed myself in learning and trying to be the best at everything. That only served to separate me farther from the group.

I developed a fear of failure and I always managed to avoid participating in anything that might prove I wasn't the best. This fear stayed with me until I opened my own business in my late forties.

One day, the teacher caught me talking and I had to stay after school. She made me write, "I will not talk in class" a hundred times. After I finished, I ran all the way home. On the way, I tore up my paper and threw it in the sewer. I was afraid to tell my mother about this incident. The shame and guilt I felt because of it was too painful. I finally got up the nerve to tell her when I was forty-five!

Can you hear?

Can you hear the pain behind the anger, the despair within the rage of thunder, or the cries of the broken heart of the hurting child within?

David, the Poet
used with permission

Puppy love, loss and guilt

Walking home from school was a thirty-minute routine that included much teasing by the boys! The boys chased the girls or irritated them in some way every day.

One boy, however, obviously wanted my attention. This rowdy youngster frequently attempted to run over me with his bike. Several times, he tried to follow me home but I would sit on the curb two or three blocks from my house and wait until he tired of his game. I was too young to be flattered. I was just annoyed! Then, one Sunday morning we heard a knock at our door. My mother answered the door and found a carefully scrubbed, redheaded, freckle-faced boy in starched yellow shirt and brown pants. The boy drew himself up to his tallest posture. "Is this where Dianne lives?" he asked. My mother said it was. Then, he sighed deeply and said dramatically, "At last I've found her!"

My heart turned to mush! My admirer only stayed a few minutes but from then on, I was madly in love with this brash, troublemaker. It was a love that lasted many years.

As a child, I lived in a garage apartment behind my maternal grandparents' house. My mother's youngest sister, Edris, still lived with them. She was only nine years older than I was and we shared a special bond. She was like an older sister to me.

Members of my mother's family and my daddy's family visited each other regularly. We all lived close to each other and we lived life at a slower pace than today's frantic race. Family time and relationships were our priority. Sadly, today's families are too scattered for close ties to develop.

When I was nine years old, my great-grandmother who was eighty-three years old died. While my great-grandmother was visiting my grandmother in the winter of 1949, she became ill. She lay in bed, too ill to get up, and no one seemed to know what was wrong. On the third day, I stopped in to see her before going to school. My mother refused to let me give Grandma a "good-bye" kiss for fear it would disturb her. Reluctant and angry, I went to school.

When I saw my daddy's face at the classroom door right after lunch, I knew instinctively Grandma was gone. I think I screamed. I know I screamed in my heart! It was many years later, during the grieving process for other losses, that I finally recovered.

Although I believe I understood the idea of death, this was my first experience with it. It hurt me even more because of what happened at the cemetery. My mother forced me to leave the safety of the car to watch as they lowered my Grandma into the earth. I will never forget the anger and sorrow I felt then. No one had thought to explain about the burial. When I realized what was happening, it was more than I could deal with. All I knew was that Grandma was supposed to be in Heaven, not the cold ground!

I soon began to act out that anger with minor behavior problems at home and school. My fourth grade class was taking a spelling test for which I hadn't prepared. The teacher always left the words on the blackboard and we were on our honor not to cheat. I was so afraid of not making a perfect grade that I looked at the board and my teacher caught me. The guilt and anger I felt over this incident devastated me.

At the age of twelve, I had another boyfriend. He was from an orphanage and we fancied ourselves very grown up and in love. We would sneak into the cloakroom at recess and steal kisses. One day, a teacher caught him going in and he refused to tell on me. He took the complete blame and received harsh punishment. We were both on the safety patrol and we were going to the national convention in the spring. Because of his suspension from the patrol program, he lost the trip to the convention in Washington, D.C. I wanted to tell on myself, but my boyfriend begged me not to tell anyone. I kept quiet because I was terrified of losing the trip and the resulting punishment from my parents if they found out.

When I entered high school at age thirteen, I thought I was grown up. I had no idea how mistaken I was.

In the middle of the school year, I experienced yet another traumatic loss. Living next door to us was a family with two children, a girl and a boy. The boy was nine years old and had developed a serious crush on me. I was tremendously flattered. We flirted with each other across the fence. My parents rarely allowed me to visit in other children's yards or homes. My mother didn't want me to make a pest of myself and she believed children should play at home, even if they had to play alone. Consequently, I was very isolated. I am sure it contributed to my perception of not fitting in.

The boy next door was Damon. He was so cute in spite of the thick glasses he wore. I felt a strong affection for him. It was not a boyfriend thing, but still I felt a kind of love for him. One day after school, he went to an old car lot to explore. He had some matches and out of boyish curiosity, he lit one and dropped it into the gas tank of an abandoned car. The gas tank exploded! The fire burned him so badly that he died that night. I never even got a chance to say "good-bye" to him. Devastated by the loss of my friend, I became depressed.

Damon's mother asked me to play the piano for his funeral because Damon loved to hear me play. Often, he would ask me to go into the house, open the window and play his favorite songs for him. It was extremely difficult to play for Damon's funeral while having to hold my grief inside. At the age of thirteen, I was *not* prepared to deal with something so stressful. Naturally, that traumatic experience added another dimension to my sense of inadequacy, loss and guilt!

When I was fifteen years old, my parents had still not told me about sex. I spent that summer with my aunt in another state, helping her care for her family after two major surgeries. Ironically, even then I was a caregiver. I enjoyed being at my aunt's house, but, I really missed my childhood sweetheart.

The boy who had found me in first grade was now my boyfriend. Although we had never dated, he came to visit me often and when he delivered our newspaper, he would stop and talk with me. One night that summer, I had a vivid dream about him. When I awakened, I was positive I was in love. I had no idea what was happening. I believed that the sensations I felt in my body had to be love! It never occurred to me to question that dream or to mention it to my mother.

At sixteen, my parents had not yet permitted me to date. A boy asked me to go to the movies once and then stood me up. Oh, did that hurt! I had cried and begged for hours to get permission to go. When he didn't show up or call, I was so embarrassed! It served to reinforce my negative self-image.

Most of the children in the grade school I had attended were from poor families. The student population was predominately children of mill workers. By comparison, my family was wealthy. However, when I went to high school the dynamics changed. Compared to the average student's family, I was poor. Moreover, I was from the "wrong side of the tracks." Making friends with the more affluent teens was difficult for me because I was shy and insecure. It seemed obvious to me that I didn't belong in their group. I masked my feelings of inferiority by becoming an exceptional student. Some misinterpreted my shyness, considering me "stuck up" and unfriendly. A few friendships developed, but I always felt I was an outsider.

Late in my junior year, my parents allowed me to go bowling once with a boy from church, and once I went to a movie with a classmate. My daddy dropped me off at the theater to meet the boy. After the movie, we went for a walk to the school stadium. When he got fresh, and I resisted his advances, he angrily told me to call my father to come get me. I told him he would have to take me home on the trolley and walk with me the mile from the trolley line. Reluctantly, he accompanied me home and I never dated him again. During the walk home, we talked about an incident at school, where David, a clumsy senior, had playfully knocked my glasses off and broke them. My date said I ought to go after someone like David who was planning to be a medical missionary. According to this angry young man, David was just my type.

Looking back, I realize that I had handled this situation very well. I had stood up for myself and demanded respect. If only I had continued to demand that kind of respect throughout the years, my life would have been very different.

Fun=Happiness? No!

When I began to understand that true happiness has absolutely nothing to do with fun, I was finally on my way to being happy.

There are three undeniable requirements for true happiness:

- Work to do

- Someone to love

- Something to hope for

For all the wrong reasons

David and I attended the same church and over the summer, we developed an interest in each other. He would walk the four miles each way to come visit me several times a week. We didn't go out because he had very little money and couldn't afford transportation. As we learned more about each other, our relationship became serious. In the fall, he went away to college and we corresponded. In October of 1957, David proposed. I accepted, of course. The following May I graduated from high school. We were married a week later.

As the wedding approached, I suspected I was making a mistake. I really wanted to marry the one I had loved since first grade, although he had *not* asked me. He was away in the Navy, after quitting school. I was sure that he would ask me when he came home. Unfortunately, my parents led me to believe that they would never permit me to marry him because of his family background. His parents were alcoholics and his mother had been married five times. Ironically, his life followed a more respectable path than mine did.

On the day of my wedding, I cried at the back of the church and begged Daddy to let me back out of the marriage. He soothed me and assured me that I was just nervous. If only he had taken me seriously, I might have walked away. If only I had listened to myself, life would have been so different!

I married to get away from home. I gave up a two-year scholarship to a junior college because I was afraid of failing. The fact that my parents didn't really want me to go was all the encouragement I needed to stay home.

I wanted to get an apartment with my best girlfriend but my parents said I would have to live at home until marriage. In those days, a respectable young woman did just that. Besides, I believed my parents could and would enforce their edict! Therefore, marriage seemed the only option left for me to gain my freedom.

This marriage lasted a tumultuous nine years and produced three sons. In it, I found the punishment that I subconsciously believed I deserved for loving my childhood sweetheart more than I loved my husband.

Yet, how could I be sure I loved either of them? When I was a teen, my mother had made it perfectly clear to me that I didn't know what love was. She said that I didn't know how to love anyone, and that I especially did *not* love her. I failed to realize that what she said was only her opinion, and not a statement of absolute fact. Unfortunately, I accepted it as fact. I also accepted as fact her assertion that I wasn't happy unless there was some kind of turmoil going on around me. Consequently, as the years went on, I allowed the turmoil to worsen until it threatened to destroy me.

Our marriage was an abusive relationship. I abused him emotionally by telling him. I didn't love him, and that I really loved someone else. He, in turn, abused me by telling me how useless and worthless I was. He would say to me, almost daily, "Why don't you just kill yourself? You say you wish you were dead, why don't you just do it and get out of my way?" This only made things worse. I attempted suicide several times, but my cries for help went unanswered. David and I separated and filed for divorce during our second year. I subsequently filed four more times before making it final.

I experienced many incidents of emotional abuse throughout the nine years of our marriage. During the last two years, it expanded to include physical abuse.

When we separated each time, I went back to live with my parents. This compounded the problem for me. From the moment I moved in, the questions started. "How could he be so bad? He doesn't seem that bad to us. What did you do to make him get mad at you?" Finally, they said, "We don't believe you! You have obviously just made this up or embellished the truth to get our attention or to turn us against David." How could I argue with their reasoning? From childhood, my parents had expected me to be perfect. Yet, somehow, I always managed to fall short. Most of the time, I felt that I was an impostor. It was either the "frying pan or the fire" for me. When I tired of one, I would just go back to the other.

So much anger had built up in me through the years that I became a destroyer. I ruined all of our dinette chairs by slamming them into the floor repeatedly. One day I picked up the vanity bench and slammed it into the floor until it broke into pieces. When I stepped back and looked at it, I was so scared of my anger that I decided right then never to show it again. Other than a few slammed doors here and there, I have kept my word. Repressing my anger, however, hasn't been good for me either. The anger I bottled up inside turned into more depression and exacerbated my self-destructive behavior. The angrier I became the more I caused myself to suffer.

I'm not sure, other than by the grace of God, how I could have survived the myriad traumas to which I subjected myself. Yet, I have taken responsibility for my choices and have taken charge of my life. I can tell you honestly that on some days it seems easy. On other days, it is a moment-to-moment battle.

Stepping out in faith

The first step in faith is the hardest. Once taken, however, Providence takes over. Unforeseen events and assistance materialize as if by magic to help you reach the goal that seemed unattainable before you stepped out in faith.

Recipe for despair

Our first son, Mark, was born almost eleven months after our wedding. We hadn't planned to have a baby so soon. Truthfully, David did *not* want him. David blamed me for the pregnancy, saying that I had deliberately miscalculated the safe period as we practiced the rhythm method of contraception because I so desperately wanted a baby. I didn't do it on a conscious level but I have to admit I wanted a baby more than I wanted anything else. Somehow, I thought to have a child would make my life perfect.

I had no idea how having a child would complicate my life. During the entire pregnancy, I had morning sickness twenty-four hours a day. After the delivery, I had what we called the "new baby blues" (postpartum depression) after my son was born.

Mark was a breech baby and he sustained injuries during the birth process. He exhibited physical symptoms from the beginning. The muscles in his legs were so tight he couldn't straighten his legs and he frequently ran high fevers. Mark's poor health put tremendous pressure on both of us. David said that if I were a good mother Mark wouldn't get sick so often.

At one point, when Mark was thirteen months old, David became so angry with me that he took a butcher knife and threatened us both. I ran out of the house with the baby and went to my parent's house about two blocks away.

Eventually, I went back to David after hearing my parents tell me how wrong they thought I was to break up our home. As luck would have it, I got pregnant. Again, it was *not* a planned pregnancy. Because of a substantial weight loss, my diaphragm no longer fit properly and it failed to prevent the pregnancy. Of course, David placed the blame on me.

During my pregnancy with Paul, our second son, my boyfriend from first grade appeared on the scene. I shudder to think of the emotions I experienced because of my feelings for this man and the stress they caused during this pregnancy. It surely must have affected my baby just as my mother's emotions affected me while I was developing in her womb.

We ran into my old flame and his fiancé in the park and stopped to talk to them. David and I became very close with them over a period of about three years. We stood up with them when they married and almost every day we spent time together.

It was bittersweet. I still fancied myself in love with my childhood sweetheart. It was further complicated because now his wife was my best friend. I know he would never have acted on the attraction that I had for him because he told me so. He said he respected me. He made sure I understood that he loved his wife and wouldn't want to hurt her. He was so noble. I hated him! No, I loved him. You get the picture. I just wanted him to love me. I really believed I loved him, but could I be sure? My mother had told me that I didn't know what love is. She said I would never know how to love anyone. This made my feelings even more confusing.

David began accusing me of having an affair with my old boyfriend. All the while David was being friendly toward my friend and his wife in person, but behind their backs, it was a different story. When I denied having an affair, David taunted me, "Why *don't* you have an affair? I really don't care if you do. You can have *anyone* you want *except* your old boyfriend!"

Recipe for despair

At one point, David threatened to call the police department where my former boyfriend worked. He wanted to cause him trouble over the affair he imagined we were having. The prospect of David sabotaging my friend's career and marriage prompted me to attempt suicide.

We had argued for hours, when, in a daze, I went into the bathroom and locked the door. I pulled the razor blade out of the package. I struggled with my feelings and finally began to cut my wrists. It was as if I were watching from a distance while it happened to someone else. When I didn't answer David's plea to open the door, he finally realized something was wrong and broke into the bathroom. He was so angry with me that he brought our oldest boy, Mark, into the bathroom to witness this terrible scene. To this day, Mark still remembers the gruesome scene and his father's comments.

David finally called an ambulance. In the hospital emergency room, I received stitches in my badly injured wrists. The doctors observed David and his surly attitude toward me during my treatment. When it came time to release me, the doctors refused to release me to David. Instead, they released me to our friends.

I hadn't learned my lesson yet. A few days later, David and I reconciled our marriage. This time, David said he believed that if we could just have a little girl everything would be perfect, so we foolishly tried to get pregnant again. Nine months later, we had another boy: Stephen. This time, however, David was disappointed, but pleased. He had wanted this baby.

The RH-negative factor in my blood caused complications for Stephen. He spent a week in the hospital and was on the verge of needing a transfusion. The doctors advised us not to have any more children. They refused to tie my tubes because of my age: I was only twenty-one. They insisted instead that David have a vasectomy.

I think the vasectomy served to increase the problems between us. David blamed *me*. He felt it robbed him of his manhood. Moreover, he still wanted his little girl. The angrier he got, the more depressed I got.

When Stephen was seven months old, I spent two weeks in a sanitarium for depression. I really hated being in there with all those crazy people. The place was a catchall for schizophrenics and alcoholics. Some people seemed normal, but they could quickly turn on you. Some patients received shock treatments and many were strapped to their beds. It was as if I were in a scary nightmare. One woman on the back hall got loose, came to my room, and attempted to choke me. Up to that point, I had refused to talk with anyone. The nurse told me that the only way off the back hall was to start talking to the doctors and nurses. Therefore, I talked to them.

Things changed after I talked to the doctor, but the situation was still less than ideal. The lack of privacy was a real issue for me.

It is no wonder that I figured out how to get out of there to save myself from those crazies! The doctor said that, to leave, I had to take and pass a test containing about 500 questions. The questions were redundant. They just rephrased them. However, I made a perfect score. I simply went through and answered all similar questions as a group. Then I made sure, when I answered the next group of questions that I didn't invalidate the answers to the first set.

The doctor took one look at the score and knew exactly what I had done. He told me he knew how I had gotten through the test, but was powerless to keep me there because of the score. This was a classic example of being "too smart" for my own good.

After I got out, I went to group therapy. It didn't work out because David refused to participate. The doctor said if David refused to attend, I would have to drop out.

Recipe for despair

As if depression were not enough, I passed a kidney stone the size of a green pea. The doctor had told me that nothing was wrong with me. It was all in my head. However, he finally believed me when he saw the stone! He had tears in his eyes when he saw how big and jagged it was. It took several weeks to pass. Besides the physical pain I had suffered, I was in a deep depression. I went to the hospital for tests and came home the next day. I was still in a great deal of pain because of the cystoscopy procedure. Yet, David insisted we go to the state fair. We walked until I thought I would drop in my tracks and David insisted that I carry the baby. He refused to help.

Eventually we decided to see a private therapist, but he only made matters worse. David had purchased a gun and he took perverse pleasure in placing dangerous objects such as knives and my prescriptions where they would constantly tempt me to use them. When the therapist challenged him about these things, David walked out and refused to go back.

Then the therapist did something terrible to me. He said, "Well, if you're going to have the name, you might as well play the game!" He said that I should at least have fun if I had to pay the price anyway. I asked what he meant by that and he blatantly suggested that I have an affair! He told me that it would lessen the pain I felt because of David's constant accusations.

I didn't immediately go out and do what the therapist suggested, but he had planted a seed in my mind. No ethical therapist would have behaved this way. It was years before I realized what a pivotal role in the downward spiral of my life he had played. Years later another therapist helped me understand that what the first therapist had done was very wrong. She said that it was especially damaging to me because of the fragile state of mind I was in at the time.

Although I didn't seek out a partner, one found me a few months later. The man flattered me. He told me I was a wonderful person and he thought I was a good mother. He said all the things I was hungry to hear, and I made the mistake of becoming involved. It lasted only a short time because the guilt nearly killed me. I told David and his reaction surprised me. My revelation devastated him. It seems that it really was *not* what he wanted to happen, after all.

When I told David about the affair, he took Stephen, who was about thirteen months old and left. He hid him away and I had to resort to legal means to find Stephen and bring him home. It took almost six weeks, but I finally got my baby back. I moved out of our home and back in with my parents after we found Stephen.

When Stephen came home, he was quite ill, and I took him to the hospital. Mark also went with me. After the doctor treated Stephen for a severe case of bronchitis, he became concerned with Mark. He had been observing as five-year-old Mark twitched repeatedly and made strange noises. When the doctor asked about his odd behavior, I told him that it had started when Mark was two years old after a fall from a grocery cart. The doctor looked into Mark's eyes and said he saw an indication that there was pressure on his brain. He wanted me to let him admit Mark immediately for tests and possible surgery. I was very frightened at the thought something so serious might be wrong and I thought I should call David. However, David denied treatment for Mark at the hospital and refused to believe anything was wrong.

In the midst of all this, we reconciled our marriage again.

Moving toward divorce

A few weeks after we reconciled, we moved to Davenport, Iowa for David to attend Palmer College of Chiropractic.

Shortly after our move, Mark fell from a high wall while riding his tricycle and it seemed to exacerbate his neurological symptoms. He also began to exhibit emotional instability.

Paul had always been a difficult child and he seemed to get worse with all the changes.

Stephen now eighteen months old, opened the car door and fell out as I slowly drove out of the grocery store parking lot. He sustained a minor head injury. He had always been just a little slow to do some things but now he seemed even slower after the fall. He didn't talk until he was three years old. God truly blessed us! The doctor determined that Stephen had sustained no permanent injury.

We made our cross-country move on a shoestring and life was *not* easy. I worked part time and David worked a full time job and went to school. When we weren't working, we were too tired to have much of a family life. This influenced the behavior of our children, who by now, were becoming used to taking care of each other.

It surprises me that, with all the anger I carried, I never abused Paul or his brothers physically. I now realize that I probably caused them emotional pain with my inappropriate teasing. However, at the time, I failed to recognize it as inappropriate. I merely teased them the way my family had teased me.

One particularly dramatic incident happened when Paul was four years old. Although he was well behaved, he and I just never seemed to get along. One day, he became angry with me. I don't remember why. He put his hands on his hips and said, "I hate you!" Before I realized what I was doing, I said, "I hate you, too!" I sent him to his room while I thought about what had just transpired.

After thinking about the situation, but not really knowing what I was going to say, I called Paul to come out of his room. As we sat on the sofa, I asked him to count to eighteen and he did. I commented on that being so many numbers. Again, he agreed. I mentioned that he had lived through four birthdays and four Christmases. I then told him that according to the law, I was responsible for him until he turned eighteen. I made sure he understood that he would have to live with me until that time. We would both have to endure fourteen more of everything. He began to get the message that if things continued the way they were going, it would be very unpleasant for both of us. I then asked him if he thought we could just be friends and help each other get through the many years ahead. After thinking about it a few seconds, he smiled and said, "Yes, ma'am." I then asked him to shake hands on our agreement like a man. To his credit and my relief, he did.

Paul kept his word. I kept mine, and from that day, we were best friends. Over the years, he was always there for me, often when he should have been playing or being a child. Late at night, when I needed someone to talk to, he was the one who came to my rescue. He saved my sanity more than once and even saved my life after I overdosed on tranquilizers.

Although this friendship was good for me, it was a monumental disservice to him. It required Paul to be an adult. I failed him because I didn't allow him to be a child. He should have been carefree, yet he had to take on the emotional burden of being his mother's best friend.

After two years of school and more fighting, David and I were ready to separate again. I worked from three until eleven in the morning. I didn't sleep well, and I had difficulty keeping up with the children and housework. Eventually, I collapsed at work. At the hospital, they kept me for several days because of complete exhaustion and malnutrition. I had hoped when I got out of the hospital that things would get better, but they didn't. A coworker had driven my car to the hospital and when they told him I would have to stay, he left the car there. David refused to arrange to have the car picked up and when it was time for me to leave the hospital, he told me to drive myself home. His complete lack of compassion devastated me. Shortly after, we separated for a few weeks. Then Christmas came and Paul begged us to try another time to make it work.

After David came back home, we moved out of our four-room apartment to a bigger place. My hours at work became more regular and we hoped things would get better. However, old habits and patterns were impossible to break. Things continued to go downhill. Even Paul, who had adopted the role of mediator, could see that the marriage would never work. The situation gradually became unbearable. I told my attorney to reactivate the divorce petition.

A month later, the divorce became final. According to Iowa law, we were supposed to have a one-year waiting period before we had the right to remarry.

After my divorce, a friend introduced me to Kenn, a younger man who immediately swept me off my feet. Kenn was different from anyone I had ever known. He was such a flirt and I felt so flattered by his attention that I couldn't resist his charms. Naïve as I was, I fell hard. Kenn was a Romeo who went out of his way to attract the attention of any female in his vicinity. He didn't attempt to disguise his interest in other women. However, he was so good with my boys that I overlooked his faults. He also was extremely protective of me. He made me feel desirable. He made me feel loved and worthwhile.

Kenn helped me to understand that it was not real love I still felt for my childhood sweetheart. Gratefully, I relegated that chapter of my life to the past. I will always be grateful to Kenn for that insight.

After a two-month courtship, we married, partly because Kenn wanted to protect me from David who was coming around and physically abusing me again. We got around the one-year waiting period that Iowa required by going to Missouri to be married. The law in Missouri didn't require a waiting period after a divorce and if we married there, Iowa would have to recognize it as a legal marriage as well.

After we married, life immediately began to get better for me. We had a loving family unit and I began to have hope. For the first time in my life of zombie-like existence, I really felt alive! I began to experience life on a different level and it was good. We went to church as a family, and, though I was sick a lot with bronchitis, we were happy.

Trouble in Paradise

As a nine-year-old girl, I had accepted Jesus as my personal Savior. I was currently active in the local Southern Baptist Church where I played the organ for church services. Kenn was a backslider in the Seventh-Day Adventist church.

After he took on the responsibility of a new family, Kenn recommitted himself to God and wanted to get back in church. We agreed to go to both churches every week, but we soon tired of that arrangement. I gave in to his wishes that we attend his church exclusively. Subsequently, I became a member of the Adventist Church. To this day, I maintain close ties to both denominations.

A few months after we married, we had a frightening supernatural experience. It occurred while I was trying to read a book about the spirit world that I had received at church. I was lying on my side in the bed, and the bed began to shake just enough to blur the words. I moved the book. Then the book began to move just enough to keep me from reading the words. I put it aside and although I felt uneasy about what had just happened I said nothing to Kenn.

We went to bed and both of us awakened sometime during the night. Although it was a hot August night and we had no air conditioning, the air felt icy cold and it smelled like a damp basement. We both felt powerless to move. As we each struggled to move our eyes from side to side, we realized we were sharing this terrible experience. It was quite a while before we could move our bodies. The hair stood up on our necks. We were terrified. We both heard what sounded like my voice, as if from downstairs, saying, My God, what a mess! As if in a dream, we both saw two priests. Their robes had gold and black circles that were trying to swallow each other.

When this unusually intense encounter was over, we managed to calm each other. We then called our pastor to come counsel with us. He thought our experience might have been a devilish encounter. He said that it could be related to the child I was carrying. We had prayed fervently for a son. We had promised to dedicate him to God's service.

A few weeks later when the delivery went well and Kenneth was born, we pushed the incident from our minds. He was a healthy, perfect baby boy! However, two months later, I became very sick. The doctor told me I had to lose weight and that I must go to a dry climate or I would never live to see Kenneth's first birthday. Naturally, I was afraid. Immediately, I started dieting and planning for a cross-country move. The doctor gave me three choices: Denver, Albuquerque, and Phoenix. We quickly decided that Denver was too cold. Albuquerque was too hard to spell. So, we settled on Phoenix.

As we were planning our move, we realized something was wrong with Mark. The doctor scared us when he told us that Mark was a ticking time bomb who could conceivably destroy our whole family. The doctor said he needed extensive counseling and that we should place him in an "only child" environment. The county, however, could *not* place him in foster care to achieve this situation without David's permission.

David, by this time, had moved back to Georgia and was about to set up his practice. He refused to give the county his permission. Instead, he insisted on taking Mark to Georgia to live. He promised to provide therapy and the "only child" atmosphere that Mark needed. At the time, I believed I had no choice but to agree and subsequently signed custody over to him.

David came back to Iowa to get Mark. A couple of weeks after they left, I found out that David had married a woman with a five-year-old daughter. His marriage took place the day after they returned to Georgia. Again, I felt betrayed. I felt so stupid for trusting David and losing my son, yet powerless to change the situation. What I had done was supposed to be for Mark's benefit. However, it ultimately turned out to be his worst nightmare. Mine too, when I found out that his stepmother was abusing him. She lacked the ability to contend with the difficulties of his neurological and psychological problems. She locked him out of the house many times, even when it was raining!

Finally, Mark told me that David was mistreating him. He wanted to come back home. Subsequently, Kenn and I drove more than nine hundred miles to where Mark was living and took him from his school. I persuaded the teacher to let Mark go to lunch with me and we promptly left the state with him. Several weeks later, the Court forced me to let David take Mark back to Georgia.

Not long after Mark returned to his father, we moved to Arizona as my doctor had suggested. My health improved immediately. Unfortunately, though, I was now almost two thousand miles away from my parents and Mark!

Although the move was good for my health, it turned out to be lethal to our marriage. We failed to find jobs for several weeks. The situation made us both quite anxious.

There we were in a strange city, with no furniture, little cash, no jobs and running out of hope! It took a full month to get our furniture delivered by the moving company. We had sold most of our possessions. The moving expense turned out to be more than we expected. We still had found no work and we were beginning to get desperate.

I asked a local church for help. I carefully explained that we had certain nonperishable items in abundance. I told them that we needed fresh milk for Kenneth who was now seven months old. We needed fresh fruits for the children and yeast to make bread. I had plenty of flour and canned meat substitutes.

I was disappointed when the woman from the church brought a small box containing only canned goods. Most items were duplicates of what I already had. Not a quart of milk or a piece of fruit was in the box! I didn't want to appear ungrateful, so I thanked her graciously as she left. I immediately burst into tears when I shut the door behind her.

A wonderful neighbor, Shirley Lovelady, came to our rescue almost immediately. Shirley just happened to pick that time for what she called a "get to know you" visit. Of course, she wanted to know why I was crying and I reluctantly told her. She told me not to worry, saying that she would return later.

About a half hour later, our Good Samaritan returned with blankets for us to sleep on instead of the bare floors. She also brought an ice chest with ice, tomatoes, butter, milk, fruit, juice and yeast! Every day, for almost a month, until we got jobs, she replenished the ice and contents of that chest. Even so, we were very careful not to take advantage. As a family, we agreed to sacrifice so that the baby could have everything he needed. Kenn and I ate one meal a day. Paul and Stephen, then six and eight years old respectively, had two meals a day and the baby had food anytime he was hungry.

When things improved for us, I went to my wonderful neighbor and asked how I could possibly repay her kindness. She told me that the only way was for us to be on the lookout for someone in need and render aid where we could. I have tried to be faithful to her memory through the years. When I do something good for someone, I always say, "You have Shirley Lovelady to thank for this!" To me, her name is synonymous with good deeds.

Heading in the wrong direction

For two years, we tried so hard! We went to church. We kept the faith and refused to quit. We worked at any and everything, from baby-sitting in a church nursery to teaching music, to cleaning schoolrooms at night. The children would go to bed at six o'clock at night and get up at ten o'clock to go with us to clean the school. They helped us empty trashcans and ashtrays and sometimes they hosed down the parking lot. Kenneth took his first steps during one of these evenings at work. We were managing, but I was becoming discouraged. I tried selling Constan cosmetics and Sculptress bras with little success.

For me, putting my thoughts and feelings down on paper had always been helpful. One day, while I was home alone eating lunch, I wrote that our financial circumstances discouraged me and I didn't see how I could continue. I hadn't intended it to be a suicide note, but when Kenn came home and read it, he freaked out!

However, unburdened of those negative emotions, I went out and made a big sale. I was eager to get home and tell Kenn.

I returned home to find chaos. Police officers were everywhere. The children were distressed and Kenn was nearly incoherent. Then when he saw me, he went into a rage. His rage wasn't against me, but directed toward God! He said we had tried it God's way and it was just not working. Now we were going to do it our way.

Things deteriorated as we walked away from God and our commitment to Him. Kenn had been working for a pest control company and the man suddenly decided not to pay him. When we attempted to collect his paycheck, the man got his shotgun, hit Kenn with it, and used it to push Kenneth and me back into the car. He threatened to kill us all. We were terrified for several days and we hid inside our home as he drove by nightly to harass us.

Then, Kenn met a new friend, Max, who invited him to go out on the town. Kenn persuaded me to accompany them to the Latin nightclub that Max frequented. It belonged to Max's uncle. Although Kenn was a party person from before our marriage, I had never belonged to the party crowd. Up to that point, I did *not* drink or dance.

We both were immediately hooked on the excitement of our experience at the club. I quickly learned to dance to the exotic rhythms of the Latin music and Kenn went to work tending bar and waiting tables.

I never had to sit unless I wanted to rest. Good dancers were plentiful and I had my pick of the best. It was as if I had been born to dance to those rhythms. Everyone thought I had been dancing for years! The old saying is true. Blondes do have more fun, especially when you are the only blonde in a room full of Latinos.

We began to go to the nightclub several nights a week. Kenn had a small photography business that we had brought with us when we moved. He began taking photos at the club between waiting on tables. That kept him busy, and yet he wanted me there always. I liked to dance and there was nothing else for me to do. I rarely sat once I entered the door. Even during the breaks, they played recorded music and someone would ask me to dance. I felt so flattered! How good it felt to be the focal point of everyone's attention! How good I felt because men seemed to want me and they complimented me constantly. Yet, it was dangerous for my marriage and ultimately helped destroy my self-esteem.

Heading in the wrong direction

It is easy to look back and say "If only…" Why wasn't I smart enough to realize that this new way of life was placing my marriage and me in mortal danger? How could I have been so naïve?

We added a second club to our list. It was a club that stayed open until four in the morning. To attend the nightclubs, we had to leave our children just before bedtime. Kenn insisted that we couldn't afford a sitter every night, so he set up a tape recorder to monitor the boys. After a few intense arguments, I finally agreed to go with him to the clubs. I reasoned that Paul was old enough to watch the others and he even seemed to thrive on this extra responsibility. I believed the boys would be fine by themselves. I continued to resist at first. However, I foolishly allowed the excitement of the music and the attention I received to sway me into making this inappropriate and dangerous choice. I am ashamed of how easily I abdicated my parental responsibility.

Soon we were going out six nights a week. The money was good, and admission was free for us most of the time. The drinking we did was on the house or bought by friends. While making our living this way, we neglected our children.

Later I came to understand how fortunate we were that nothing terrible happened to our children while they stayed home alone. We were lucky the county was not involved. They would have taken the children away from us. Perhaps Kenn and I were naïve. We had always lived in safe neighborhoods free of crime. I had grown up in the south where one trusted people. Kenn grew up in Davenport where it was much the same. We felt safe enough to leave our doors unlocked and our keys in the car. We just assumed our children would be fine. However, I now understand what I failed to realize then. Children should never be left unattended!

Mark was still living in Georgia with David. Paul was ten and Stephen was eight. Kenneth was now two. Paul was in charge. He carried the responsibility of an adult. The tape recorder monitored the boys and we listened to it the next day to see if they had behaved.

Of course they behaved. We were raising them in the era when parents expected obedience from their children and they got it! My boys knew if they didn't behave, a spanking would follow. We only had to tell them to do something once. They knew all too well what would happen if they didn't. Second chances were rare.

Our new way of life influenced us to see other people as much more attractive and more desirable than we found each other. I never lacked for admirers. Neither did Kenn. Several times, I saw him exchanging kisses and embracing with other women.

Kenn's obsession with sex, fantasy and open marriage was a disease that had now overtaken me as well. However, even after insisting on an open relationship, Kenn never admitted that he was unfaithful to me. On the other hand, I again chose infidelity. The result was the same as with David. When it happened, Kenn discovered that wasn't what he wanted after all!

I thought it was different this time, but it wasn't. It just came cloaked in a different disguise. It was still an attempt to run away from my problems and to punish Kenn for the way he had treated me. For, by this time, Kenn was as ugly to me as he had been good before. Not physically abusive yet, but the emotional abuse was escalating.

We began family counseling because the teacher had caught Paul stealing in school. It was his cry for help because of what was happening at home. I believe he was acting out because of the heavy load of responsibilities he carried and the tension in our marriage.

Counseling only served to make us both realize how miserable we were. Things escalated to the point that we began to argue in public as well. We got into a serious argument at the nightclub where we were working. One of my regular dance partners came to my defense and rescued me by taking me out of the club before my husband could become violent.

What a mistake it was to go with him. Better to have listened to whatever my husband had to say and then walk away in an honest separation. However, in the heat and fear of the moment as Kenn began to get angry, I did the wrong thing. I feared he would become violent. I realize that fear is *not* an acceptable excuse. At least two hundred people were there. If I had been using my head, I would have realized that someone would have come to my rescue.

When my friend took me home the next morning to collect my children, I slipped in and picked up Kenneth. Kenn grabbed his shotgun and followed me to the street. He held the shotgun to my stomach as I held the baby. He threatened to kill us both if I did *not* leave without Kenneth. Paul and Stephen were looking on from the yard. Kenn told me I could *not* take them either. He discharged the gun at my feet to show me he was serious. After a few tense moments, I handed him the baby, got in the car, and drove away.

To this day, my youngest son tells me that he remembers the shotgun episode in vivid detail. Reading this manuscript has helped him to work through residual feelings about this and other events. As a teenager undergoing counseling for behavior problems, he came to realize that, as a small child, he had perceived it as an act of abandonment on my part. He hasn't determined why he did *not* see his father's part as abandonment. However, he mentioned that he has felt abandoned by his father at other times.

I left with my friend and he dropped me off at a motel. The following day I went to see an attorney. By this time, however, Kenn had taken all three boys and left the state. He drove to Iowa and contacted an old school friend of his in Illinois. He offered to allow his friend to adopt

Kenneth if he and his wife would promise never to let me see Kenneth again.

While Kenn was transporting Kenneth, now almost three years old, to his friend's home, he left Paul and Stephen sitting on the steps of a church. They were alone in a strange city and he knew they could *not* tell me where to look for their brother.

When Kenn returned to Arizona, he brought Paul and Stephen with him. He later returned them to me, but he adamantly refused to tell me where Kenneth was living.

Shortly after they returned, Paul and Stephen went to Georgia to visit David. While they were gone, my attorney advised me to do whatever it took to find out where Kenneth was. He told me to get Kenn to call our son. He wanted me to get a phone record for him to trace. I went back to Kenn and followed my attorney's advice.

A few weeks after having left Kenneth in Illinois, Kenn suffered a mental breakdown. He began having alternating episodes of depression and fury. He was like a man possessed by a demon. He began going around trying to destroy all the gold circles in our house. You many remember the shared supernatural experience from several years before where black and gold circles were trying to swallow each other. That incident seemed to relate to what we were now experiencing.

Nothing was safe or sacred. He cut our wedding rings. He cut the circular gold braids on the lampshades into pieces. He had a tie with a design composed of circles. He cut every one of them. He began to paint everything in the house gold to protect us, he said, from the demons he thought existed inside him. He burned all of his pictures because he said he could see the demons looking out from his eyes. We pleaded with the demons to leave him and Kenn's face would shrivel, as if he were suddenly very old. He would then start shaking and eventually fall down. A few moments later, he would revive and be okay.

We became afraid to enter the house or stay in it without carrying an open Bible in our hands. We truly believed that we were under a satanic attack. It may have been another satanic attack or simply hysteria brought on by all the anger and tragedy we had experienced. Whatever it was, I never want to experience anything like it again!

During the worst of it, Kenn began to abuse me sexually. At first, I encouraged him in his rough treatment. I believed that I deserved the punishment he was inflicting. As the abuse escalated into a daily ritual of sadistic cruelty, I initially fought against it. However, I quickly sank into despair. I reached the point where I had no will to leave. Instead of fighting, I now became a willing victim and allowed the cruelty to continue. I got up, went to work, and acted as if nothing was wrong. At the end of the day, I came home to more cruelty. Once again, I began to feel like a zombie. The kids were gone. We were completely alone. No one was present to stop our insane behavior.

After two weeks of physical abuse, I finally manipulated Kenn into calling to find out how Kenneth was doing. We found out that our little boy had been very sick. I immediately told Kenn that my attorney had put me up to tricking him. I said that now we could put a trace on the phone call. Now that I had accomplished this, I told him that I was leaving. Kenn then told me where Kenneth was staying and I borrowed the money from my parents for an airline ticket so I could bring him home. Kenn and I tried to smooth things over and make a new start. However, it was much too late for that.

Shortly before I went to Illinois to get Kenneth, Paul and Stephen came home. We kept up the pretense of a mended family and went to the airport together. It was my first flight and a bomb threat delayed the flight. My plane left after four hours of anxious waiting. The friend who was meeting me at the other end was frantic because they refused to tell her what was wrong. She thought we had crashed. A bomb scare is *not* pleasant even for a seasoned traveler, but for a novice it was especially frightening. I was a nervous wreck to begin with and a walking disaster by the time I reached my destination.

My father-in-law took me to pick up Kenneth. My baby was in a state of shock. He wanted nothing to do with me. As I approached him, he called the other woman "Mommy" and ran to her. It broke my heart to see him this way. During our return trip on the plane, he cried out to everyone else and called for his mommy. I was distraught and embarrassed. I fabricated a story to help me deal with the situation. I told everyone that my sister and her husband had died in an accident. I was taking their son, who had never seen me before, home to live with me. Somehow, I got through the ordeal. Imagine my dismay when we arrived at the airport and he jumped from my arms and ran to Kenn crying, Daddy, Daddy, Daddy! I just wanted to die.

As we tried to put our marriage back together, we sought more counseling, this time through the church. It was too little and too late. I insisted that if we were going to divorce Kenn would have to file. I did *not* want another divorce. I wanted to heal our marriage, but the trust was gone. Although I forgave him for what he had done to me, he could *not* forgive me. He filed for divorce and it was soon over.

When the divorce was final, Kenn left town and went back to Iowa. I was so lonely. I needed him and I spent a small fortune on long distance calls trying to persuade him to return to me.

A matter of life or death

Rather than have my tubes tied after Kenneth was born, the doctor had used an IUD to keep me from getting pregnant again. Shortly after my divorce from Kenn, I had the IUD removed because I was having a problem with excessive bleeding and pain. The doctor told me that I had an infection. He gave me an antibiotic, a prescription for pain, and sent me home.

Two days later, I developed a fever and pain in my whole body. I called in "sick" at my office. I assumed I had the flu. The company nurse where I worked had referred me to the doctor who removed the IUD. When she discovered I was sick she told me to see him again.

I told her I didn't want to expose all those pregnant women to the flu; I would be all right. Two days later, I was still unable to get out of bed. When the company nurse called again, she told me that either I find someone to take me to the doctor or she would send a company guard to take me.

A friend from across town came and took me to the doctor's office. The doctor wouldn't speak to me as he examined me, except to say that he would talk to me after he finished the examination. I dressed and went into his office.

The doctor said, "There is no easy way to tell you. I'm not sure I can save your life. The infection has spread throughout your body. You must admit yourself to the hospital immediately and prepare for major surgery. You have no time to delay! When you get there, call your attorney. Find out how to draw up a will to take care of your children and your possessions. Call your parents and tell them to come. Arrange for someone to care for your children until your family can get here. Most important of all, pray!"

The doctor's words stunned me! I was only thirty years old. I wanted to die, but not like this. I wanted to live, but not the way I had. "Please, God, help me!" I cried out in my heart.

I followed my doctor's instructions. I wrote out my will. I also called Kenn and begged him again to come to me. He said that if I were dying of cancer he would come. I told him the possibility of my dying during surgery was great. He still refused to come back. He said he didn't want to waste his money on a trip just for my surgery. I didn't need to hear that. I wish I hadn't.

There I was, with three young children, in a city almost two thousand miles from home and my parents. I was alone. The physical abuse I had suffered had ravaged my body. What little self-esteem I had regained was rapidly evaporating, and now I thought I was probably going to die!

I remember the doctor's words just before going under the anesthesia. "I'm going to do my best to save your life, and I brought along someone to help me do it," he said. That was the last thing I remembered until I woke up in recovery.

By this time, Mother had arrived. The doctor placed me in isolation for two weeks. My infection turned out to be Staphylococcus, probably caused by the abuse I had suffered a few weeks before. The infection had slowly spread, and after the removal of the IUD, it suddenly exploded inside me. My uterus had filled with pus and burst, as had one ovary and both tubes. The other ovary was about to burst. That had caused endometritis, and peritonitis. The doctor removed a small section of bowel as well. He said I was lucky to have survived.

As psychologically damaged as I was already, this additional trauma to my body and to my spirit completely crushed my self-esteem.

Although I was a mother, now I could never have another child! I felt cheated in a way that only one who cannot have a child can understand. Having babies was about the only area of my life that I considered successful. Now, I'd lost that! Kenn made it clear to me that he considered me "damaged goods." No respectable man would want me now. It only occurred to me as I wrote this book that perhaps David had felt much the same when he had his vasectomy.

Soon after I got out of the hospital, a friend introduced me to her friend's father. His name was also Ken. That was difficult for me to deal with. He very quickly took over my life and was very good to me. It was the first time a man had been so kind to me, and I didn't know how to deal with it. Consequently, I did everything I could to push him away, but he stayed.

As I recovered from the surgery, the new Ken in my life hovered over me and tried to take care of me. He was good to my children. He wanted to marry me and buy a big house so each child could have his own room. I was terrified! I thought he felt sorry for me and I didn't know what to do, but I agreed to marry him.

In spite of the severe setback in my life that the surgery caused, I had such an instinct to survive that it amazed my doctor. He told me later that he hadn't expected me to make it through the surgery. He didn't expect I'd be well enough to go dancing a few weeks later!

I went dancing because I craved attention. I needed someone to hold me and I longed for validation of myself as a person. In my mind, I imagined Ken just felt sorry for me. Besides, my relationship with him didn't seem romantic to me. His teeth were in pitiful condition. He needed a lot of dental work and I couldn't bring myself to kiss him.

Unfortunately, when I did go out, I went alone and without Ken's knowledge. At the nightclub, three weeks after the surgery, I met someone who would further destroy me.

By this time, you are probably thinking, "How stupid could she be?" However, I was hurting physically and emotionally, and I continued to make poor choices.

I went dancing and I met Tony the first night. He was a gorgeous young Latino. Dressed in a pinstriped suit and with bushy hair, he attracted all the young women. After I danced a slow dance with him, Tony made it clear that he was *not* going to leave me alone. He was very attentive and particularly cautious because of my recent surgery. Tony was new to the club and the younger women were unhappy that I had his undivided attention. At thirty years of age, they considered me an "old" woman. Tony wanted to see me again and I agreed. The next day, there he was and he stayed in my life for several years.

I quickly broke off with the wonderful caring man who had wanted to rescue me. Unfortunately, I was *not* ready to quit being a victim. Two months after we met, Tony and I were married. Subsequently, I discovered that he was an illegal alien. I realized, too late, that marriage was a part of his plan to get a green card. Once he had achieved that goal, his attitude toward me changed.

After the marriage, it became more difficult for me to tend to my family. Tony made it clear that he thought the boys should visit their father until the summer time. David had sent Mark back to me shortly after the surgery because he and his wife were having so much trouble with him. Even so, at Tony's urging, I agreed to let all three boys visit with David for the remainder of the school year.

That left me with Kenneth, now a four-year-old. It also left me more tied down, because I had lost my built-in baby-sitter. I eventually came to realize that this was just what Tony had counted on. He immobilized me so that he could come and go as he pleased without me knowing the extent of his activities.

Tony had always been sexually overactive. Eventually, I came to the realization that he was having sex with someone different almost every day. This was hard for me to understand. Three to four times a day he made love to me. Why wasn't that enough? What I didn't realize was that Tony was a sexual addict.

In spite of the physical excesses, he was extremely gentle with me. He was also very good to Kenneth, and with this much physical attention, I rationalized, how could I feel unloved or unwanted?

A few months after we married, my kitchen caught on fire one night. Alone at home, I was cooking dinner. Tony had taken Kenneth with him to visit a friend. When they returned, the fire was out. Tony took me to the emergency room where I received treatment for third degree burns on my arms. I had blisters that were unbelievable and it was incredibly painful, but I had to continue to work. Instead of being considerate of me, Tony seemed to go out of his way to insist I do things for him that caused pain in my arms.

A few weeks later, he took my car one night and wrecked it. The car was in the shop for about six weeks. He took the loaner car that the insurance company provided for me and drove it to Mexico. He left me at home without transportation and I had to ride my bicycle five miles each way to get to work for a whole week. When he returned, I found marijuana in the car and we fought. He became abusive at that point. Initially, the abuse was verbal, then escalated to pushing and shoving and finally he hit me.

I told Tony to leave. I then went out, bought a Great Dane for protection, and filed for another divorce. Tony was gone for good, I thought.

Forgiveness

Forgiveness is *not* an emotion. It is a choice. Forgiveness *cannot* undo the damage. Forgiveness is only attainable through mercy. While important to the transgressor, forgiveness is vital to the happiness of the person wronged.

I can't believe he took the kids

Summer was upon us and the kids were coming home! I was planning for their return. When I contacted David about their return, he stalled and said he had something special planned for the Fourth of July holiday and they could come home after that. I reluctantly agreed and began looking forward to that time.

Shortly before the end of June, David served me with papers charging me with abandonment of Mark, Paul and Stephen. According to Georgia law, I had abandoned my children. I made the mistake of allowing them to reside in the state for more than thirty days without a written agreement. I almost lost my mind when I realized I might lose my children. Surely, this could *not* happen! The thought of it was more than I could bear!

I arranged to go to Dalton, Georgia for the court date. I drove two thousand miles, stopping only to buy gas or food. Kenneth and my Great Dane, Tim, accompanied me. On the way home, I stopped in Louisiana for gas. The station attendant insisted I stay for a little while to rest. I parked the car and put the dog outside. He was restless and I stepped outside the car to check on him. I stepped in the middle of a fire ant mound and received almost a hundred stings! Of course, rest for me was now out of the question. I got back in the car and continued on. Three days later, I had to make the return drive. Again, I stopped only when necessary.

The year was 1971. Miniskirts, big hair and the new morality were the norms out west where I had been living. I drove home to the south where life was more like it had been in the fifties. I had no idea that the judge would look at my hair and my choice of clothes and decide I was an unfit mother. I also didn't count on having to compete with David's second wife who had unexpectedly returned. Her conservative suit only made me look more out of place.

My children had previously told me that their stepmother had left and filed for divorce. It stunned me when she showed up and said she wanted to be their mother. The boys had written letters telling me their father had mistreated them. They wanted to come home. I had their letters in my purse to prove it. Foolishly, I still thought regaining custody of my boys would be easy.

The local counsel that my attorney had secured for me wasn't adequately prepared. He was more interested in trying to seduce me than anything else. He seemed to think that the hearing would just be a formality. He told me I would get the kids and it would be over. "This was a time when men just didn't get their kids unless their mother was unfit," he said.

I lost my parental rights in about ten minutes. We met in the judge's chambers while the boys sat in the courtroom. They didn't allow me to speak to the boys before I went in to talk with the judge.

The judge refused to look at the letters from the children, and refused to listen to my attorney or me. He accepted everything David said as truth. David was now a prominent, influential doctor in Dalton, Georgia. His wife told the judge that they had been having problems but had resolved them and she was home to stay. She was anxious to be a mother to these children. The judge believed her. She was so convincing that even I believed her! The judge ruled in their favor and I walked away with only locally supervised visitation rights. This meant, of course, I wouldn't see them for a long time because I lived on the other side of the country. Because I had once taken Mark away, the judge refused to allow the boys to leave town to visit me under any circumstances. He didn't even allow them to travel a hundred miles to visit my parents if I was going to be there.

You can imagine what this turn of events did to my almost nonexistent self-esteem. My children were the last vestiges of my identity and my last link to reality.

My parents, grandmother, Aunt Edris and I gathered at a motel in Dalton for my last visit with the boys. It was incredibly painful for us all.

When I returned to my home in Phoenix a few days later, I was half-crazy with guilt, anger, loss and fear. I was in no condition to argue with Tony, who now insisted on coming back home. Therefore, I let him come back, but I said I would *not* marry him. I figured he would be gone again soon enough anyway. At least this way, I wouldn't need another divorce.

Within days, I discovered that, in spite of what David and his wife said in court, she had packed up and left the next day. This time they made it permanent. This turn of events made it even harder for me to accept what had happened. The judge's reasoning seemed ludicrous to me, but I had no funds or means to try to change the circumstances.

I learned much later that Stephen had suffered the pain of perceived abandonment by me that day in the courtroom. He was too young to understand that it was the judge and his father who were forcing me out of his life. Before Stephen went to stay with his father, I had given him a stuffed toy to take with him. Years later, he showed the toy to me. It was very worn and tattered. He told me that he used to cry himself to sleep while holding it. He would talk to it and pretend that it was his mother.

My heart broke to hear of the pain that he had endured because of my stupid mistakes. It hurt even more because I knew firsthand how that pain felt! It was tragic that my children now felt the same feeling of abandonment that I had felt as a baby.

Strange as it may seem, I believe the pain we have endured as individuals, and collectively as a family, created a special bond. Because we each have experienced the same kinds of pain throughout the years, sometimes together, sometimes alone, we now have a common bond and empathy for each other's feelings.

Going home

A few weeks after Tony came back into my life, he insisted that I sell my house so we could move into a rental house closer into town. I could never figure out his reasons for wanting to make that move unless it was to make me feel less secure.

After about three months of his running around and leaving me alone, I developed such severe abdominal pains that I thought I was going to die. I was in the emergency room more than once. The doctors couldn't find anything definitive. At work, a heavy door had hit me in the head when someone opened it quickly and I developed severe pain in my face. The doctor thought it might be a brain tumor at first so I underwent several tests. The doctor finally diagnosed the pain as trigeminal neuralgia.

It was becoming impossible to deal with all of the pain and losses. It was hard to think rationally. I finally decided I had to move back to Georgia so that I could at least see my children regularly. My father had laid a guilt trip on me for not coming home immediately after I lost custody. He didn't let up on me until I decided to quit my job and go home.

I thought going home to Georgia would help me get rid of Tony, but he surprised me by refusing to let me make the long drive alone. He was worried because of the winter storms I would have to pass through. Therefore, he drove me home and we got even closer on that trip. It was like the early days and I thought that maybe he would be different when we got home. After a few days, he began to talk of staying in

Georgia with us. He said he realized that if he went back to Arizona he would probably never see me again.

When we arrived, it surprised my parents to see that Tony had come with me. However, they agreed to let him stay in their basement apartment until he decided if he were going to stay permanently. Problems existed from the beginning. My parents refused to tolerate our intimate relationship under their roof. They firmly insisted that if we were going to continue that kind of behavior we must get married. I felt powerless to say no to them. If I refused to honor my parent's wishes, they told me we would have to leave.

In retrospect, I don't think my parents were wrong to expect me to honor their values in their home. However, if they had fully understood my emotional condition, perhaps they would have handled it differently. If they had, perhaps I might have found the strength to walk away from Tony.

This was one of many choices I made throughout my life that did *not* seem like a free choice at all. They were more like "rock or a hard place" alternatives.

Therefore, we got the blood tests, and married at the courthouse. My parents insisted on seeing the marriage certificate to prove we had really married. Nine days later Tony was gone!

I now had no husband, no divorce, no job, and only Kenneth instead of all my boys. Additionally, my parents were telling me what to do as if I were a child! They wanted me to get another divorce!

I bounced back, filed for a divorce, got a job and life went on. Again, I sought comfort anywhere I could find it, which was in the dance halls. I was *not* a drinker. I was a dancer. I loved the music and the high it gave me when I danced the night away. I lived for those nights of dancing. Then on alternating weekends, I would drive a hundred miles to visit Mark, Paul and Stephen.

David was saying things that made me think that we could get back together. Although I was tempted to reconcile just to regain custody of the children, it would never have worked. My lack of self-esteem and my wild lifestyle had changed me too much. I was no longer innocent and naïve. I was wise with respect to my experiences, but not enough to put a stop to it. I was not wise enough to formulate a successful plan to get my children back. Therefore, when Tony wrote that he wanted to come back to me and start over, I dropped the divorce petition and welcomed him back into my life.

I set strict limits. He could no longer borrow my car. I would give him no money. He would have no more nights out with the boys or girls. He accepted the terms. Things were good for a few months and we had a wonderful summer. We went camping with the boys. Since I had officially moved back to Georgia, David now permitted them to come for a summer visit.

By the end of the summer, Tony had gotten enough money together to buy his own car and the problems started again. Only this time it was worse. He insisted we move from the big house where we lived into a small apartment. With Tim, my Great Dane, getting so big, I knew it would be hard, but I foolishly went along with it anyway.

Children had teased Tim when he was a puppy and he hated all children except my boys. He would try to bite a child any time he could. Less than a week after moving into the small apartment, some children were playing noisily outside when I took Tim out for a walk. I told them to sit still because the dog would bite. However, one little boy ignored my order and got up. Tim pulled me to the ground, got away from me, and mauled the little boy. He tore the boy's chest and thigh open. I thought the dog was going to kill him. I was terrified. Tim was so big and restraining him was almost impossible for me. Finally, I got him under my control and the boy ran home.

The boy's father rushed him to the hospital and he recovered. However, I immediately called the police to come and destroy the dog. It was almost like giving up a child. He was so close to me and so protective. It was a very emotional time for me. I blamed Tony because of the move and myself for going back to him.

Even then, I knew he was seeing other women. In desperation, I bought a gun and picked him up after work one day and held the gun on him for about an hour. Fortunately, I did *not* have what it takes to kill someone. However, the incident served its purpose. It scared him enough that he was ready to call it quits. A few days later, I found him in bed with another woman and he pretended that he was unaware of her presence. Even I wasn't dumb enough to buy that one! Now, it was definitely over for me as well. I filed again for a divorce.

Finally, it was over. I only saw him a few times after that. In spite of all that had happened between us, he would show up on payday to give me a few dollars to buy milk for the baby. Although Kenneth was five years old, Tony still called him the baby. Tony once asked to come back. I wasn't emotionally strong enough to resist him. Fortunately, he changed his mind a few days later and disappeared from our lives.

A few months after my divorce from Tony, David married his third wife, a patient of his. She was a younger woman, who had two small children. She and I never got along. At least his second wife and I were civil to each other. Again, another woman was in charge of my children, and she tried to prevent me from seeing them.

How could I have done that?

I became involved with a man I met while working my second job. Although I tried several times to break off our relationship, he stalked me relentlessly and threatened me with violence if I left him. I believed him when he said I would never escape from him. He once told me that he had murdered several people in the South African country from which he had immigrated. He told me his father was Pakistani and his mother was from India. He said that explained why he was so mean.

I didn't know he was married until much later in the relationship. When I found out about his wife, he told me he was trying to get a divorce and take custody of their little boy. He persuaded me to help him with the attorney and paperwork. Then he took the boy to Canada to live with his parents as a ploy to prevent the child's mother from seeing him.

I am mortified that I could have helped him do such a cruel thing, especially after having had the same thing done to me. Unfortunately, my attraction to this man was secondary to my fear of him. Consequently, I did anything he told me to do.

In the middle of my affair with the "stalker," which lasted almost two years, David's wife called me and told me that David was abusing Paul and Stephen. She said that if I would meet her half way between Atlanta and Dalton, she would return them to me.

My father went with me to pick them up. David had pinched their fingers with pliers for misbehaving in the car, but I think David's wife had done the most damage. Now, she just wanted them to leave!

During that summer, I was on leave from my job at the hospital because of an injury I had sustained in a fall at work. The child support was so little and irregular that applying for food stamps was necessary for me. Almost every month I had to file papers just to get the monthly child support check. Besides his trying to hurt me by delaying the support payments, David would promise to see the boys and break his promise.

Earlier that summer, he had let Mark come to see me for a short visit. When I saw the bite wound from a brown recluse spider on Mark's leg, for which David had refused treatment, I exploded. Mark decided he wanted to file charges against his father for neglect and I permitted him. He was fifteen at the time. David never let it go to court. He just gave up and Mark came home to live with me.

Shortly after Mark came home, I took him to a neurologist to see if we could find the underlying cause of his problems. We discovered that Mark had Tourette syndrome and three other specific movement disorders. The doctor prescribed medication for Tourette and his emotional problems. Tourette is a disorder characterized by bizarre twitching, noises and repetitive behaviors that are uncontrollable when awake, but absent when asleep. Those who are not familiar with the disorder naturally assume the child is acting out or just seeking attention.

Now, for the first time, I understood why Mark had been such a problem. I realized his bizarre movements and shouted expletives were not "behavior" problems. He had a neurological disorder. Both David and Kenn had punished him for his odd and annoying behavior. I had tried to cope with his tics. However, it was often too much for me as well. It was especially difficult when coupled with all the other problems in our lives. Our failure to understand that Tourette was the reason for Mark's bizarre behavior had caused him to develop emotional problems. Although we were partially responsible, from Mark's perspective, his first stepmother did the most damage to him. It left him with an overwhelming hatred for women in general.

Later that summer, David had promised to send bus tickets for the boys to visit him. The tickets didn't arrive in time for the trip. The failure of the tickets to arrive made Mark angry and then he became depressed. He took an overdose of two of his medications. If it hadn't been for my experience as an admission clerk working in the emergency room of a large trauma center, Mark would have lost his life. As it was, we got him to the hospital with only moments to spare. He remained unconscious for more than forty-eight hours. David refused to take my emergency call from the hospital. In anger, I informed his receptionist that one of his sons was dying and it would be up to him to find out which one! That got David's attention, but still he didn't come until much later that night. His excuse was that he had an office full of patients that he had to treat.

When Mark, then sixteen, came out of the hospital, the doctors thought it best for him to live with my parents. Now at last, he would have the "only child" environment he had needed so many years earlier.

Just before this latest crisis, I had broken off with the married man and thought I was through with him. Then, after a few weeks, he began stalking me in the hospital parking lot after I got off work. I was very frightened. So much so, that I let him back into my life. At least then I knew where and when to expect him.

In the early fall of that year, I began to have trouble with Paul and Stephen. While they lived with their father, a man in their community had molested them. I later found out they weren't the only ones. Some parents ran the man out of town, but never prosecuted him. They didn't understand the damage he had done to their children. No one understood except the innocent children who were involved.

Tattoos of the Heart

It seemed that I was losing control of everything. Day to day life with all its problems became overwhelming for me. I eventually turned to Kenn for help.

Kenn seemed to have his life back together. He was studying for the ministry, and we had graduated to friendlier terms. He had remarried and adopted his wife's two boys. I asked him if Paul could live with them for the rest of the school year. Kenn said yes, so I took him to Michigan to live with them in September. I turned over the portion of child support that was for Paul and paid his school tuition for church school.

In October, Kenneth was very lonesome for Paul. In reality, Paul was more of a parent to Kenneth than I had been. Stephen was having difficulty with his added responsibilities for Kenneth. This was his first experience at being in charge and it was more than he could handle emotionally. Kenneth began putting pressure on me. He wanted to go to live with his dad and Paul. Again, I called Kenn and asked if he could help me, and he did. Kenneth went to Michigan.

In early December, Stephen, an only child for the first time in his life, suffered depression. He was lonely for his brothers. He began acting out. While I was at work in the evenings, he slipped out of the house to hang out with his friends. Soon, he was getting into trouble. Stephen said he wanted to go live with his brothers so I called Kenn again and he said to bring Stephen right away.

Christmas was very lonely. Still, I found the strength to go on.

When I took Stephen to be with his brothers, I did not make the trip alone. The stalker went with us. He was still invading my life. He was not yet finished with me!

Losing my children again devastated me. I could not understand how I could have let it come to this. I poured myself into work. I had two

How could I have done that?

jobs. I sent the extra money I made plus the child support from David to help provide for my boys.

Mark was on an emotional roller coaster and I got frequent calls from my parents to come out and try to reason with him. I never had a peaceful moment. I felt guilty over the loss of my boys. Mark was going through so much. Moreover, the stalker would *not* leave me alone.

After a few months, David caught on to why the kids no longer came to visit him and why they were always out and had to return his phone calls. He insisted on regaining custody. I had no financial resources to fight him and I believed I had no choice but to let the boys help decide the issue. They knew what it was like to live in all three homes and so I asked them where they wanted to live. Stephen was the first to say he wanted to stay with his dad. Then Paul reluctantly agreed. With a heavy heart, I went to Michigan and signed the papers to change custody.

Much later, I found out that things were not as pleasant at Kenn's house as I had thought. The boys had a hard life there because Kenn and his wife were extremely strict.

My repeated attempts to extricate myself from the affair with the stalker were unsuccessful. I finally agreed to accompany him to Canada to visit his son and we stayed for several weeks. During this time, he began to push me to drink. He had always used threats and physical abuse to coerce me into doing whatever he wanted. I hated the taste of beer so he bought Champale because it had a milder taste. He forced me to drink a third of a bottle. He kept after me until I could drink a whole bottle. Then he insisted I drink more frequently. Once I could handle a six-pack of Champale, he started me on Michelob. It is a miracle that I didn't become an alcoholic. By the time we came back from Canada, I was drinking two six-packs a day and he was drinking a case.

At the time, he also took diet pills, which increased his abusive tendencies.

Before we went to Canada, filing bankruptcy had been necessary for me because he had maxed out all my credit cards. I ended up losing my new car and everything I had except my spinet organ. He had insisted I sell my piano before we left. Then he pocketed the money.

I had taken a leave of absence from my job at the hospital to go with him to Canada. When I wanted to return to my job after the leave was over, he refused to bring me home. Unfortunately, I had no funds to travel on my own.

Consequently, when we returned from Canada several months later, I had no job and no funds. He got work immediately and we continued as before, with one exception. I had decided I wanted out, no matter what! I accidentally hit upon the ideal way to get him to leave me. I made myself as undesirable as I could. I gained quite a bit of weight and I began to curse and argue with him. This was so repulsive to him, it only took about three weeks and he was ready to call it quits.

It took a few weeks for me to recover from what I had become, but eventually my life began to change. I stopped drinking, lost the weight, got a job and began to get on with my life. It was extremely lonely, and though he had moved out, the stalker came around to torment me whenever he felt like it.

Noel, Noel, Noel

Noel, Noel, The angels say
For Christ is born on Christmas Day!
Awake, ye shepherds and tell the news.
Christ Jesus came to save the Jews!
Noel! Noel! Noel!

Arise! Go tell of the Savior's birth
And spread the news through all the earth.
The wise men following yonder light
Will be here soon, this very night.
Noel! Noel! Noel!

And lo, the babe in the straw he lay
While all around him knelt to pray
Their thanks to God in the Heavens above
For this, the gift of God's great love.
Noel! Noel! Noel!

Rejoice! Rejoice, this lowly birth
Brings joy and hope to all the earth!
Go, shepherds tell it while angels sing.
A babe is born as Christ our King!
Noel! Noel! Noel!

Missing You

How have I missed you? Let me try to say:

I missed you when the phone rang and your voice was not the one who spoke to me.

I missed you when I needed to bare my soul to someone and no one cared enough to listen.

I missed you when I saw the rain and it brought back memories of a cherished past.

I missed you when the day's work was finished and the loneliness settled like a shroud over my mind.

Sometimes, even in the midst of being busy, I missed you!

And that is when I realized just how important you really were to me!

My baby comes home

After living with his dad for about fifteen months, Kenneth came home. This time, I thought, "I will do a better job of being a mother." At first things were wonderful. Kenneth was now seven years old.

After I left the stalker and moved into my new place, he continued to bother me. He came to my new apartment and raped me while Kenneth was in the other room. He threatened to kill Kenneth and rape my mother and all the women in my family if I didn't give in. As afraid of him as I was, I gave in. Finally, when he saw that he had broken my spirit and killed my desire for him, he left me.

As much as I loved my son, I still could *not* get my life together. I still needed the attention I could get on the dance floor. Therefore, I left him alone several times at night and went out dancing. As I look back, I cannot believe I was so stupid and self-centered and so oblivious to the dangers of leaving him alone.

The job I had at a doctor's office was barely adequate. Then I lost that job and all I could find was a temporary position that paid even less. It barely paid the rent, and I had to rely on food stamps to feed us. I could no longer afford a sitter during the day. School had just let out for the summer and Kenneth had to stay by himself. Although he was *not* supposed to leave the house, he did, and promptly got into trouble. The sheriff called me at work several times to tell me that my son was getting into mischief. He was putting pennies on the railroad tracks and generally making a nuisance of himself in the apartment complex where we lived.

I had no prospects for a permanent job and I panicked. Kenneth kept telling me he thought he should go back to stay with his father because he thought it was too hard for me with him there. Again, a child who should have been busy being a child had to act like an adult. His comments to me should have given me a clue, but I didn't learn until much too late, what was really going on in his heart.

I contacted Kenn about taking Kenneth back until I could get on my feet. His wife refused to allow it unless I signed over custody to them. She said that it was too disruptive to their household when Kenneth came and went so casually. Perhaps it was. Kenn and I later realized she demanded this of us to either to keep Kenneth away or to get me out of the picture completely.

After much discussion with them, to no avail, I realized I had no choice but to agree. I reluctantly went to the office where their attorney had forwarded the custody papers for me to sign. On the way there, I talked with Kenneth at length about what was happening and he was adamant about going back to his father.

The attorney explained the finality of the decision to us. I tearfully signed the paperwork. When we reached the hall outside the attorney's office we were both crying. The reality of the situation had finally sunk in for both of us.

Kenneth and I went to the car and as we were getting in, he broke down and sobbed. He told me that he really did *not* want to leave me. He had only insisted on doing it because he thought it was the best thing to do for me. He thought it was too much of a burden for me to take care of him. What a heartbreaking experience for a child! We both felt trapped by the circumstances, and the future seemed hopeless.

Overcoming this setback was incredibly difficult, but I vowed that things would change.

I promised Kenneth that I would telephone him every other week and that I would write to him weekly. I promised him that I would never give up our dream of being together again. We would always have this promise between us. When we talked over the phone, I would say, "Don't forget the promise!" He knew what I meant. Those four words gave us both the courage to get through the next three years.

As luck would have it, within two weeks after Kenneth left, I found a secure job paying the best salary I had ever made. How guilty I felt that I had not figured out some way to keep him until I could support us.

A few months after the stalker walked away from me for good, I ran into his former brother-in-law by chance. We started talking and he told me that he and his sister never blamed me for what happened. They knew her former husband had probably threatened me. I subsequently went with them to court and testified in an attempt to have the child returned to his mother. The judge delayed his decision and the case dragged on for months. By the time the judge ruled, the child had started school. He said it was in the best interest of the child not to uproot him from the only home he had known since he was six months old. With heavy hearts, we all gave up. His mother decided not to appeal.

Although the child's mother had forgiven me, how could I forgive myself?

Through all of this, my new neighbors, Marcus and Wendy, sustained me. They were the first to tell me how incredibly strong I must be. It seems I was not as weak as I had imagined. They pointed out that I had survived so much and was still functioning. When they got married that summer, they recited the following poem I wrote for them while I played the music I had written to go with it for their wedding. They were the first racially mixed couple I had ever known and I came to love them dearly. Marcus and Wendy are still together more than twenty years later. How I envy that kind of lasting relationship!

We, Lovers, Friends

Joy of my heart, friend of my mind
I'll never grieve you, for 'tis true, love is kind.
Love is a look. Love is a touch.
Love is a whisper that you love me so much.

Others would try, desperately try, hoping to see us break.
Fierce though their efforts be, stronger the bond they make.
All through life's cold dark night we'll stand side by side,
And when the dawn shall surely break, they'll know we've
    turned the tide.

For love is victorious, and victory is ours!
No longer slaves are we to any earthly powers.
Free now to live our love honestly,
And all the world is ours.

We, Lovers, Friends surely have won
the right to call our spirits free.
Set free by the love of a friend.
Set free by a love with no end.

Rejected!

Marcus and Wendy had introduced me to Alex at one of their parties. Although he was thirteen years younger than I was, we had a lot in common. We loved music and dancing. We started dating, but our relationship only lasted a few months. Alex wanted a relationship with someone who needed him. When I didn't need him constantly, it made him uncomfortable in the relationship. As I began to heal emotionally and become more independent, and less needy, he became less interested. Consequently, when I fell and injured my ankle and managed to get myself to the emergency room instead of calling him late at night, he coldly walked away from me.

His leaving devastated me. It hurt me in a way I had never before experienced. This time, I knew for sure that I had done nothing wrong. *His* insecurity caused the breakup.

I was accustomed to being the one to end a relationship, and my fragile self-esteem suffered yet another blow.

As before, I turned to poetry to vent my emotions. I just wanted to stop hurting.

Rejection

I was a butterfly: Golden! Alive! Fluttering through life.

You could have captured me and preserved my beauty for all time—you with your net of love and caring.

Yet, you chose to let me fly free of entanglement in that net you wove about me as you teased me.

Now as winter comes, my colors fade and I become but dust upon the earth, a memory in your quiet times, and, I am lost to you forever.

The final rejection

I was a butterfly, fluttering through life. You captured me with your net and made promises, unkept.

Butterflies need sunshine, flowers and freedom. Instead, you enshrouded me with gloom and the sickly sweet smell of freedom unattained.

Were I nourished and cherished, I would have fanned the cool breezes against your fevered brow. I would have danced for you in the sun. I would have been the prize of your collection.

Yet now, I tremble and writhe in agony, my wings torn from my body, no more to fly, my appendages broken and useless, my sensory devices plucked out. Yet the pain still surges over me, around me, through me!

Still, the mercy of death does *not* come.

On being content

Fun is transient and does *not* equal happiness. True happiness only came as I learned to be content no matter what the circumstances.

In the depths of despair, I sank even lower

I decided to go to a church singles' group whose advertisement I had seen in the paper. I was interested in attending the group because they dealt with failed relationships. It sounded like just the thing to help me recover from this latest loss.

I attended a meeting, but it just didn't live up to the advertising and I didn't plan to go again. As I left the meeting, a man I had met earlier in the evening approached me. He said his name was Sam. He was 6 feet 6 inches tall and looked very awkward. He asked me for a date, and I refused. He pressed me for my phone number. After about twenty minutes of trying to get rid of him, and not wanting to be rude, I foolishly relented and gave it to him.

Sam then began a concentrated campaign to get my attention. He called me several times a day. He came and stood outside my window. For several weeks, he continued to pester me until I gave in and let him come inside for a visit. He considered this our first date. What a mistake it was to let him into my home!

Sam now began to court me in earnest. At least that's what he called it. He called me at work on both of my jobs to make sure I arrived safely. If I were late getting to work, he was frantic. He called to say hello on all of his breaks and at lunch. He checked on me just before I left work to tell me to be careful on the way home. If I failed to arrive as quickly as he thought I should he would panic and come to my home to wait for me.

It became impossible to separate from Sam. He threatened to destroy himself if I refused to marry him. My feelings of responsibility for him terrified me. Yet, I felt helpless to abdicate that responsibility because of his mental condition. It frightened me to think that he might hurt himself. I didn't have the heart to walk away from him. I was afraid he would commit suicide. It didn't occur to me until much later that Sam was stalking me.

Like a fool, I gave in to Sam's pleadings and married him. Afterward, I learned from his family that Sam had sustained brain damage during a difficult birth. He was a man who was more like a six-year-old boy. He couldn't read or reason with the complexities of the world. Yet, in spite of his disability, he had held the same job for many years.

I should have realized what a mistake I was making. However, I didn't want to hurt Sam or be responsible for him destroying himself. I reasoned that it would be like murder if I left him and he killed himself. I reconciled myself to endure the marriage as my punishment for all my other sins.

Our marriage lasted only six months. I became overwhelmed with the attention Sam needed. He required constant help to navigate the maze of life's decisions and everyday living. I felt I was going insane.

A few days after we married, my maternal grandmother passed away. A few weeks later, his grandmother passed away. She had been the one bright spot in our relationship. Without her, I no longer thought I could deal with Sam and his mother, who was also mentally unstable. I decided to use the same tactics that had worked so well on the *other* stalker. I wanted to make Sam leave me. It worked! Why, oh why, didn't I think about doing that before marriage?

Again, in an attempt to ease the pain and loneliness, I began going out by myself. The only place I was interested in was a Latin nightclub where I could dance to the exotic rhythms of Latin America. It was there that I met Marco. He had come to Georgia from Ecuador several years earlier. He was a very smooth dancer and we were drawn to each other immediately.

In the midst of all of this, Kenneth came home for a visit. While he was visiting, I took him ice-skating where I had arranged to meet Marco. When Kenneth fell on the ice and broke a front tooth, Marco came home with me to make sure Kenneth would be okay. When I insisted on going alone to take Marco home, this was the final insult to Sam. He could take no more and he finally left. He filed for a divorce the next day.

A few months after our divorce, Sam married a teacher. Several months later, his mother passed away. Less than six months after she died, he died following gallbladder surgery. I felt guilty that I had treated Sam so badly. Yet, I don't believe I would have survived if I had stayed with him.

Life is too short

Don't waste it on anger or worrying over what could have been.

This time, the light at the end of the tunnel was not an oncoming train!

Within a week after Sam moved out, Marco moved in. At Marco's suggestion, we decided to move closer into town and we gave up my cozy apartment for a bigger one that was much older. Now, instead of being two blocks away from my work, I had to travel about thirty minutes. I wasn't very happy about that but we got along so well I thought I should compromise.

Marco encouraged me to pursue my dream of being a professional musician. Years earlier when we lived in Iowa, David had prevented me from playing piano with a group of retired professional musicians who had asked me to join them.

Then, years later, I was set to audition for a restaurant in Phoenix when I had to come back to Georgia to fight the custody battle with David. I had to miss the audition and when I returned to Phoenix, they had already filled the position.

Now, with Marco's support and encouragement, I called the Holiday Inn in downtown Atlanta and arranged for an audition. The Food and Beverage manager hired me on the spot and I started the gig three days later. I worked five nights a week in their restaurant playing an electronic organ and singing. It was a wonderful experience, but working two jobs at a time was getting hard. Eventually, it became more than I could handle and after eighteen weeks I had to give it up.

Although Marco had told me he would never marry me, he changed his mind a few weeks later. At Christmas, he proposed and our simple wedding was on New Year's Day. Marco said he wanted to start the year right! This wonderful man listened to the sad story of my past. He told me in his broken English, "Just because you have lived in the gutter doesn't mean you can't get up and walk on the sidewalk. If you choose to walk on the sidewalk, I will be proud to walk by your side!" What a man! We truly loved each other, but, tragically, we came from different worlds that would prove impossible for us to merge successfully.

We had been married only a couple of months when Paul called late one night and told us his stepmother had thrown him out of the house. We immediately went to Dalton to get him. I was worried about how things would work out with a teenager in the house along with my new husband. Marco assured me that everything would be fine.

Marco got along very well with Paul and having Paul with us made life more interesting. I appreciated having at least one of my children home again. Since Paul had been my good friend for so many years, it was especially meaningful to me.

A few months later, Kenneth, along with Troy, one of his stepbrothers, came for a visit. Immediately, Troy, who was the same age as Kenneth, began causing trouble. Seeing they had favored Troy over Kenneth was not difficult. He wanted his way constantly. I realized that I couldn't depend on Troy to settle down and follow the rules at our house. I called Kenn and said Troy would have to go home.

We sent Troy home and things began to settle down. Kenneth, now ten years old, told us his stepmother and her sons often mistreated him. The two boys dominated Kenneth, and because Kenn was gone so much of the time, he did not see what was happening. Kenneth told me he loved his father, but really wanted to stay with me. The time had come for me to "keep the promise."

This time, the light at the end of the tunnel was not an oncoming train!

When I called Kenn to tell him that Kenneth wanted to stay with us Kenn insisted on speaking to Kenneth. When Kenneth told his father that he did *not* want to come home, Kenn became angry and he said many hurtful things to both of us. He told Kenneth that he no longer loved him, and never wanted to see him again. He told me that if Kenneth stayed with me I would have to agree to leave the custody agreement in place. This way, he wouldn't have to pay child support. Kenn said it would be even better if Marco would adopt Kenneth. He said he was willing to give up his parental rights.

As much as Marco cared for him, he believed that adopting Kenneth would be wrong. He was sure that eventually Kenn would get over his hurt, but an adoption would make reconciliation more difficult. Therefore, Kenneth stayed without Marco adopting him. We now had two sons and no child support. Paul worked part time while he was finishing school and helped as much as he could.

We moved to a new apartment. We picked that particular location because it was next door to the church school I wanted Kenneth to attend. Although we really needed three bedrooms, we had to settle for two. Kenneth and Paul constantly bothered each other because of having to share a room. To alleviate the problem I separated them by creating a spot in the corner of the dining room for Kenneth.

The stress of all the changes was overwhelming. My job situation was stressful because I was working in a travel agency where 48 of the 50 employees were smokers. I was allergic to the smoke and I developed asthma because of the extreme exposure to cigarette smoke. As if this were not enough, Marco stopped taking tranquilizers. Then, he cut back on his alcohol consumption. The combined stresses on both of us took an enormous toll on our relationship.

My face wore a perpetual frown due to the smoke exposure and tension. I wasn't angry, but Marco thought I was. This upset him to the point that he could no longer deal with it. We had words and he walked out. I honestly thought he was gone for good so I packed his clothes and had them waiting by the front door.

Two days later, he returned and saw the boxes. Seeing them hurt him deeply. He had returned with the intention of staying and trying to work things out, but when he saw the boxes, he just walked away.

In spite of all that happened, Marco and I continued to be friends. We saw each other often. He continued to help me financially. Best of all, he finally managed to get off the pills.

Marco had been very instrumental in the improvement of my relationship with my parents. He had been quick to insist that I go back to church although he seldom went. After our separation and divorce, I continued to attend church. I began to work in earnest on my relationship with my parents.

Marco and I still believe that we saved each other's lives and we have a bond that lasts to this day. Some twenty years later, we still send birthday and Christmas cards to each other, and Marco always sends me a Mother's Day card. He moved to New Jersey a couple of years after our divorce, but we still keep in touch.

Life begins at "forty"

Shortly after my divorce from Marco was final, I moved into the house on the church property next door. My life was turning around and I became active in church again. Even with the stigma of another divorce, I was beginning to recover some of my self-esteem. This time, I didn't blame either of us, and I moved on without sinking into a deep depression. What progress I had made! For the first time in my life, I was learning to be alone. I had come to realize that to live *with* someone I must first learn to live *alone*. Relationships built around the kind of neediness I had exhibited most of my life had failed.

As my fortieth birthday approached, I contemplated the saying "life begins at forty." As I thought about it, I began to examine myself to see if I could diagnose and fix the problems that had plagued me for so many years.

Realizing that I was the problem was the first step. I felt I had reached the critical moment. I had to make a mid-course correction in my life! Accepting that, and setting about to right the wrongs was the beginning of the "rest of the story." No longer being satisfied to run away from myself and hide in failed relationships was the second step toward taking charge of my life.

It was no longer enough for me just to go with the flow. My life had to change so that I could become the person God had designed me to be. I was truly blessed when God answered my prayer for patience. As a bonus, He also gave me the ability to empathize with others. With this newly found strength and wisdom, I began to make major changes in my life.

For most of my life, I thought my parents would have been happier if their first baby, Paula June, had been the one to live. I thought God was wrong when he allowed my sister to be stillborn instead of me. However, I know in my heart that God doesn't make mistakes!

My birth was *not* accidental! My parents did *not* create me! God created me only when they gave Him the opportunity. He did *not* permit me to die when I was sick with scarlet fever and diphtheria! He did *not* strike me dead, as my mother suggested He might! He did *not* permit me to take my own life, although I tried several times! He did *not* allow me to die when I was thirty years old and had to have emergency surgery to save my life!

I began to realize that God had been there through it all! He had brought me through all these experiences as I went my own willful way. He was the one who didn't permit me to lose my sanity. He permitted me to become who I am today by letting me experience the hard life I chose. I gladly give God the credit for the underlying strength that saw me through what many others might not have survived.

I had reached at a point in my life where I had to draw a line between the past and the present. To have a promising future, I had to declare that the crises in my life were over! I didn't die! I was still alive! I was no longer a victim! I was a survivor!

I buried everything from the past that I couldn't fix in the depths of God's love. I buried every disgraceful secret, every rejection, my fears, and failures, so that I might live my life to the fullest.

Through the years, as I shared parts of my story with friends, they encouraged me to write a book. As this manuscript slowly emerged into that book, I realized they had been right! I do have an important story to tell, and it might help someone in their struggle to change their life's circumstances. My friends suggested that my story could possibly influence the choices of some young woman about to go astray, or encourage someone who is trying to overcome a painful past.

What I didn't consider, is the profound effect it would have on my sons. I was afraid they might be ashamed to see my life's story in print. Never, did I imagine the overwhelmingly positive response I was to receive from the two youngest. It has helped them, as adults, to understand events in their lives that they could *not* comprehend as children. Because of those traumatic events, they each have gone through their own emotional problems. This book has been especially meaningful to Stephen, who told me, "This book validates my feelings, my life! You have to tell it to others." He also urged me to publish this book under my real name. He said it would be a witness to the distance I have traveled and the profound changes that, with God's grace, have taken place in my life. Using a fictitious name would make it impossible for me to use this book as my testimony to help others on a more personal level. After thinking about it, I knew he was right.

I had never given myself a chance. I had always looked for someone else to lean on. In the process, I had always chosen the wrong kind of person. I realized that in every relationship I had been involved in, that I had always been a giver. They were takers. I vowed never to look for a man again, and I didn't. I even commented that if I ever had another relationship, it would be because God sent someone to my doorstep! Then, I set about learning to live by myself and with myself.

I stopped actively searching for someone to share my life. However, my gut feeling was that this was *not* going to be the end of it, and, it wasn't.

All my life, I had resisted failure, mostly by refusing to attempt difficult tasks. Yet, for all of my adult life, I thought I had been a failure at everything, especially relationships. The one thing I knew in my heart was that I couldn't survive another failed relationship.

Attitude adjustment

Life is 100% what happens to us and 90% how we react to it. Stay in charge of your attitude.

The ultimatum

A few months after we moved into the new house, Paul got a job and moved into his own apartment. Things went well until he lost his job and had to move back in with us. The loss of his job devastated Paul. Depressed, he stopped looking for work. He just moped around the house. I tried everything I could think of to get him moving and nothing seemed to work. The situation was deteriorating beyond my ability to handle it so I issued an ultimatum, "Get a job or get out!"

He chose to get out. He lived in his car for three days until he realized he had to do something about his situation. He joined the reserves and went to basic training. It was the best thing he could have done for himself. At the end of basic training, he was selected *Soldier of the Year* by the local newspaper and they rewarded him with a trophy. We were all so proud of him.

Fortunately, the ultimatum I had given him was just what he needed. It was the impetus that pointed him in the right direction. When he finished basic training, he set out to learn the picture framing trade. He made quite a reputation for himself and became very successful.

For a few months, things moved along, enabled by the momentum we built up in our lives. I was working a day job and doing freelance word-processing at night and on weekends. For the first time in my life, I was at peace with myself. Content to be by myself, I was *not* looking for anyone to fill a void. I felt no void!

Analyzing my life experiences up to that point had begun to give me incredible insight. For the first time I began to take complete responsibility for my part in the tragedies of my life. In taking that responsibility, I was building stepping-stones to a brighter future than I had ever dared hope to experience.

Trying to make some sense of it

In retrospect, I began to realize that when I was a child I had no control over the incidents that helped to shape the adult I became. Now, I was an adult. It was completely up to me to decide who I would be. I was becoming mature and wise enough to make appropriate choices. Previously, I had plenty of opportunities to make better choices, but I did not. Now, it was time for me, with God's help and direction, to bring my life under control. It was unfortunate for my children that I didn't gain this insight earlier in life.

I now clearly understood that if I had practiced my religious beliefs I would have taken a far different path. Why, you may ask, didn't I? The only reasonable answer is that the poor choices I made were a willful way to assert my independence from my parents and those in authority. I might have rebelled less if I had believed that my feelings and opinions counted. Unfortunately, I didn't know how to speak up and tell my parents that I needed that kind of validation.

I was born to moderately poor parents, into a family with a small vocabulary and little education. The word "feel" was only one of many that we used inappropriately. That misuse served to heighten an awareness of my feelings. I mistakenly depended on feelings to guide me through life. Real progress in getting my life under control began only after I learned to lead with my brain instead of my feelings.

As a child, I received mixed messages from many sources, and I did not have the capacity to sort it all out. In church, I learned to follow the Ten Commandments. I heard the preacher tell me to love my neighbor. However, as I watched the congregation put that into practice I realized the caveat was if they were the same color or if they belonged to our denomination.

I also learned in church that marriage was supposed to be for life. However, they didn't tell me what to do if a relationship became abusive. They said nothing about counseling nor did they encourage me to protect myself. They just didn't talk about those things. Men were supposed to treat their wives as Christ would treat the church, and women were supposed to be submissive. *And, that was that!*

At home, I learned by observation that marriage was a permanent arrangement. I also learned by watching my parents that being in control was okay for the wife. I didn't know how to reconcile this with the Bible's charge that a man should be the leader in the home. These weren't my first mixed messages, but perhaps they were the most influential.

Then, although they practiced fidelity in my family, the soap operas were on every day. Even as I was growing up in the fifties, the soaps were full of immorality. Watching them was even better than hiding and reading the most popular women's magazine of the day: *True Confessions*. Everything was big as life on the screen. Of course, back then they still left a lot to the imagination. However, they teased and tantalized in an attempt to trigger the imagination so we would want more of the same. Now, soaps and other entertainment mediums have evolved to the point where they leave almost nothing to the imagination.

Many fine, upstanding church leaders watch such shows. I once read a comment about television that is so true, "People who watch television willingly allow strangers to come into their living room and do despicable things. They permit these strangers to do things that they would never allow family, friends or neighbors to do in their presence."

Trying to make some sense of it

We've all heard the saying, "Monkey see; monkey do!" When my children watched the Three Stooges and started hitting each other as they had seen on television, it stunned me. I realized that in the past I had been a monkey! I had seen it all and I had done it all. Now, to my dismay as I watched, my children were becoming monkeys as well.

Although I learned the right things at home and at church, the morally corrupt scenes imbedded in my impressionable mind through television were a contradiction. If you hear something, you may forget it, but if you see it, you will remember it. Moreover, if you see it often enough, it will make an impression on your soul. Even the Bible says, "By beholding, we become." Yet, we wonder why our children have behavior problems!

Don't take me wrong. This book is not about how television ruined my life. However, I harbor no doubt that it influenced me in ways that do *not* make me proud. When asked to describe my life I used to say, "Take three soap operas and mix them together and you may have an idea of what it has been like." Thinking back on that makes me want to cry. Even in later years, I allowed myself to slip into the old habit of watching my favorite show. Sometimes I would ask friends or my mother about various characters in the show from time to time, just to keep up. Many characters had seemed like family to me. With the arrival of the VCR, I was totally hooked again as I taped them and watched them at night.

After hearing a particularly moving sermon about the damage this kind of entertainment can do, I gave up the soap operas permanently. The strength to give them up was an answer to prayer and a deliverance for which I will always be thankful. While I lived in the world of make-believe, I had great difficulty in solving personal problems. The mentality I had developed was that we should resolve everything in a few episodes. I had also learned from the programs that without major crises, life was boring and mundane.

Children, who haven't developed a tolerance for enduring life's annoyances, quickly learn from television to expect immediate resolution. When real life hits them square in the face, and they can't quickly resolve a problem, it further sets the stage for a sense of inadequacy, failure and low self-esteem.

Right on my doorstep

Having said that the only way I would ever have another relationship would be if God delivered someone to my doorstep, God did just that!

It happened while I was living in the house behind the church. I also attended services there regularly. However, as a divorcee with a past *and* a tattoo, I felt uncomfortable and lonely much of the time during the services. The congregation was ultra conservative. They did *not* approve of divorce. I felt out of place at the social activities, but I kept going anyway.

Paul, an older Hungarian gentleman, began coming to the church services. He seemed as lost and lonely as I felt. Even Kenneth noticed how lonely he looked. Having experienced the isolation for ourselves, we could empathize with him. Kenneth and I reached out to welcome him. Paul appeared to be an "outsider" as we were, so we sought to include him in our group of two. I experienced no romantic attraction to Paul. I considered him a lonely, little old man and set out to do a good deed by befriending him.

I found out that Paul came from a similar background to mine. He had been married four times. He was still married to his fourth wife but separated for more than a year. His first wife lived in another state. She was the mother of his son who was a year younger than I was. His second wife had passed away after having drunk herself to death. His third wife lived in Florida after having taken everything Paul had brought into the marriage. His fourth wife had a young child by a previous husband and they had played upon Paul's need for love and attention. She married Paul, applied for his Social Security benefits for herself and her son and then shut Paul completely out of their lives. While still married to Paul, she went to live with her first husband and subsidized their household income with the newly found social security money.

Broken and lonely, Paul left Florida and came to our community to be close to his son. They had little in common except multiple marriages.

When I reached out to Paul, I didn't anticipate that he would be so desperate to have a successful relationship. If I could have seen what was coming, I probably would have run the other way. Seeing him with his need so painfully exposed was, for me, like looking into a mirror of my past.

A few weeks after we met, Paul asked me out on a dinner date and I reluctantly accepted. I didn't want to hurt his feelings by refusing, but I wasn't interested in anything beyond a friendly relationship. Paul was sixty-nine, twenty-eight years older than I was and I couldn't imagine him being interested in more than a friendship either!

As it turned out, Paul was a delightful person. I enjoyed being with him. He really knew how to entertain. He took me to expensive restaurants. He made me laugh! Most important of all, he treated me with the utmost respect.

What is even more important, Paul was an instant hit with Kenneth, now the only one left at home with me. My other sons really liked Paul as well. I enjoyed watching my son as he thrived on the attention Paul paid him. It was a natural progression as their friendship grew into a deep love for each other.

After only a few dates, Paul proposed to me. It was a total surprise to me and it was something I definitely didn't want to hear. I had no clue the relationship was headed in that direction. It upset me greatly because I had never considered Paul in a romantic way. Paul did *not* attract me. Although he was charming in his European way, he just wasn't my type. I believed that Paul had fallen in love with Kenneth first, I was just part of the package.

Knowing my sons' collective opinion about me getting seriously involved with anyone else, I decided to let Kenneth participate in my decision about getting married again. Now that I was getting my life in order and my priorities straight, I decided to put Kenneth's welfare ahead of mine. I was sure he would *not* want me to marry. I thought this would be a graceful way to exit the relationship. What a coward, I was! I didn't have the guts to decide for myself. I was afraid to say no and didn't want to say yes. I didn't want a repeat of the emotionally forced marriage I had made a few years earlier. I had vowed never to let anyone manipulate me into choosing someone with whom I had no bond. However, this time, the potential for developing a bond was present. I just hadn't seen it!

I told Paul that if he asked Kenneth and he agreed then we would talk about it further. I thought that would scare him off. He was afraid, but not enough to change his mind. About a week later, he got up the nerve to ask Kenneth what he thought about us getting married.

Kenneth, a master of pregnant pauses, hesitated for several moments. Then sighing, he said, "It's okay with me on one condition." Immediately, Paul's courage departed. He had no way of knowing what was coming next. Nor could I have ever imagined that my son would say, "If you will adopt me and let me take your name, then you have my permission. I want us to be a real family." Paul was so touched that he cried. Cayce and I hugged him and each other.

I decided to follow through with my commitment to put my son's welfare first. I saw how much Kenneth wanted this marriage and I believed it would be good for him. It wasn't exactly what I would have chosen for myself, but then, my previous choices were disappointing!

A few months later, we were married. Two months after the wedding the adoption process was completed. We all cried again as the judge told us that Kenneth was now Cayce Paul Feyer. His birth name was Kenneth Charles and his brothers sometimes called him KC. He had chosen the name Cayce because it sounded like his initials. He took the name Paul to honor his new father and his brother, whom he loved so much.

My marriage to Paul was much like an old-fashioned arranged marriage. Sometimes, however, those marriages turned out to be the most stable. Perhaps it was because two people went into marriage without infatuation, learning first to like and then to love each other.

Shortly after our wedding, I realized that this marriage was going to change my life in ways I could never have imagined. The choice I had made was going to help me continue to mature. However, it didn't take long for me to realize that I had bitten off a big chunk. It was going to take a lot more effort to digest the changes in my life than I had anticipated. I had discovered soon after the marriage that Paul was as insecure as I had been and his self-esteem was almost nonexistent. He told me that he only felt he existed when he was interacting with someone else. He needed someone constantly. Now that someone was I!

Paul had always needed to be the focal point of everyone's attention. He came from a home where his older brother was the favored son. His parents thwarted him at every turn, discouraged him constantly, and made him believe he would always be a failure. Paul's failed marriages and a distant relationship with his son only served to magnify his sense of personal failure.

Paul had suffered lung cancer some twenty years earlier. About three years before I met him, he had undergone surgery for prostate cancer. The surgery had rendered him impotent. That was especially difficult for him since he already had such low self-esteem.

Paul told me at the beginning of our relationship about his impotence. Honestly, that was acceptable to me, as I did *not* find him physically attractive. I believe that if our marriage had required sexual intimacy I would *not* have married him.

A marriage without sex appealed to me. I thought that it would help me distance myself from the destructive behavior and relationships of the past. Distinguishing between love and affection was becoming easier for me. A marriage with affection but no love was tolerable.

What I hadn't bargained for was the loss of affection as well. Paul was not openly affectionate, nor could he handle my affection for him. I have always been a very affectionate person. I was uncomfortable with Paul because I couldn't show affection to him without him pushing me away. I can't remember a time when I was lonelier than this. Here I was, in a marriage with no affection except in public. Paul always had to show off his younger bride by making affectionate gestures and comments about his virility.

I had always been an emotional eater. Now, it began to get out of hand as I struggled to cope with the myriad stresses in my new life with Paul. I gained weight and my health deteriorated. I tried diets and pills. They would work for a short time, but when my emotions were out of control, I'd just start eating again. In desperation, I sought help through *Overeaters Anonymous*, but even that wasn't enough. This destructive pattern of behavior lasted many years. I even used Fen-Phen! Fortunately, I was luckier than many who used that deadly combination. However, I sustained enough heart damage to qualify for a small settlement.

In later years, I learned two important elements necessary to bring my compulsive eating disorder under control. I learned that the foundation for success is proper and adequate nutrition. Powdered whey mixes work quite well for those of us who don't want to swallow a dozen pills every morning. The mixes provide amino acids and vitamins. The second aspect of gaining control was learning to "feel" my feelings instead of trying to bury them with food. Once I learned that pain and other emotions do *not* equal hunger, I could focus on my feelings and work through them. I no longer ate candy bars to suppress my feelings! I no longer carried that burden, but, I had to remain vigilant. I had to practice this on a daily basis. Otherwise, reverting to old patterns of eating would be easy. I slipped often at first, but now, only rarely.

Another problem began to surface. When we went shopping if I said, I like that, it would magically appear for me at home. This now became a relationship that brought me material things. I wasn't accustomed to getting things and it made me even more uncomfortable. It seemed as if Paul was trying to buy my love and me. He made a big deal out of giving me something new to replace everything anyone else had ever given me. He insisted I get rid of practically everything anyone else had ever bought for me. I kept almost nothing from my past life except photographs. It made me feel as if I had prostituted myself. When I had accepted his proposal, I had no way of knowing it was going to be like that.

Some of you are now thinking, What is so hard about receiving gifts? What is so difficult about having a husband who gives you everything he thinks you want? I tell you it was hard for me! A part of me thought I didn't deserve it. I didn't want to feel that he was trying to buy my love and the anxiety I felt was a high price to pay.

When Paul and I first met, he told me he had retired and was living on a fixed income. What he didn't say was that his brother was an internationally known musician who had given him a substantial monthly allowance for years. He didn't tell me that he really wanted to go back to work. Paul's level of self-esteem seemed to relate to his success at work. He had managed hotels from New York to California, and Puerto Rico. When he stepped down from managing, he became a

Controller for a country club. After that, he bought a small motel unit and managed it for a few months.

Paul went back to work about a month after we married and changed jobs three times during the first three years. He was still working when he passed away almost eight years later, at a job he had held for about five years.

Paul also didn't tell me he was a compulsive spender. He brought in more money in a month between his three sources than I had been used to seeing in any six-month period. However, with his penchant for dining out in fine restaurants several nights a week and traveling, we were soon deeply in debt.

About three months after we married, my first grandchild, a boy, was born. We went to visit him when he came home from the hospital. We were driving through a terrible rainstorm and although I was driving cautiously, I hydroplaned and lost control of the car. Fortunately, we escaped serious injury, but this became another trauma to overcome as we struggled to learn to live together.

The one bright spot in our lives was our new grandson. We watched with delight as he grew. He had red curly hair and a very sweet disposition, at least until the terrible two's.

Diversion

No! Sonny, Don't do that!
Look HERE, Sonny, see the cat!
No! Sonny, don't touch this!
Come here, Sonny, give me a KISS.
No! Sonny, NOT on the rug!
GOOD BOY, Sonny, give me a hug.
No! Sonny, PLEASE don't cry.
Come on, Sonny. Go BYE-BYE?
NO! Sonny, not right now!
LOOK, LOOK! Sonny, see the cow!
No! Sonny, you might FALL!
Come ON, Sonny, let's GO play ball.
No! Sonny, don't pull MY hair.
Come on, Sonny, let's get YOUR bear.
No! Sonny, it's time to go back.
Its time for YOU to hit the sack.
No! Sonny, you CAN'T stay out!
Come here, Sonny! PLEASE don't pout.
NO! Sonny, give me your cap.
Come on Sonny, let's take a nap.
No! Sonny, please GO to sleep!
Don't let me hear ANOTHER PEEP!

Back to work

A few months after Paul and I married, I had to have extensive foot surgery. It was extremely difficult for me to go back to work after I healed. I was used to staying at home and I liked it. I wasn't looking for a job. However, an employment agent I had known from before solicited me for a job that she thought would be perfect for me. She was very insistent. Several months earlier, while I was working as a freelance consultant, I had typed a book of legal forms for her ex-husband. She called me several times and was most persuasive. Reluctantly, I went to the interview. Although I didn't want to go back to work, I put my best efforts into the interview, and I got the job!

This new job came with much responsibility and more demands than I had ever experienced in a job before. To say that it was stressful dealing with this new job simultaneously with my marital problems is an understatement. However, the new position offered opportunities and challenges to grow that I couldn't resist. The company specialized in "Change Management," something I had never heard of. However, I had spent my entire adult life creating and managing change, although very poorly.

The mechanics of positive *Change Management* were fascinating. I gained tremendous insight into my personal life as I learned about how to manage change in the business world. I learned how I should have handled the circumstances I had dealt with over the years. It taught me how to develop the inner strength I needed to maintain my marriage commitment. It gave me a new determination to overcome the obstacles in my way.

Although I really liked my new job, the strain of being constantly committed began to tell on me. We lived close to my office. I had no transition time between one commitment and the other. At the office, I gave more than a hundred percent because they required it. At home, Paul expected the same level of commitment from me as well. When it seemed to be more than I could handle, I talked to Paul about quitting my job. By now, however, he had come to depend on my income and he didn't want me to resign.

As time went on, it became even more difficult to live with Paul's need to interact with someone constantly. That meant he needed me to share everything with him. His idea of sharing everything meant that I must eat when he ate. He took it to the extreme, becoming offended if I did *not* eat the same kind of food. When I succumbed to his wishes regarding my diet, it was detrimental to my health. Food sensitivities and addictions coupled with the stress I was enduring exacerbated the compulsive eating. Yet, he failed to understand that it was destroying me. If Paul watched television, he insisted I watch, too. It wasn't enough for me to be in the same room and read a book or newspaper. If he read the paper, I had to read the paper. If he wanted to talk, I had to talk. His opinion was that unless we were doing the same thing simultaneously, we were *not* together!

Loneliness for myself overcame me! I was totally lost in the confusion. I had no time alone. I began to understand how important private time was to my sanity.

Along with that, I was severely sleep deprived because Paul was a restless sleeper and I was a light sleeper. For several years, I had used a sound machine that provided white noise so that I could block out other noises. Eventually, we had to use separate beds and finally separate rooms for me to get the rest that I so desperately needed.

Cayce was now a teenager. I had little energy left after dealing with Paul to focus on him. Cayce had been hyperactive as a child and experienced problems with school. He never seemed able to complete his homework. He barely got by, but only because of his excellent verbal skills. Later, we found out he had been learning all along. When he became a junior, he suddenly began to make A's and B's. The psychologist who worked with him said his brain had just needed to catch up.

Then came the awful day when Paul found a bag of marijuana in Cayce's dresser drawer. I had pleaded with Paul several times to allow Cayce to have his privacy, but Paul simply wouldn't listen to me. Now, because Paul had found the bag of pot, it put me in the position of having to address the issue with Cayce. Consequently, I flushed the marijuana down the toilet and issued an ultimatum to Cayce: No drugs in our home!

What worked with my son, Paul, did *not* work with Cayce. Cayce chose to leave home rather than follow our rules. This crisis created even more tension between my husband and me because we couldn't agree on how to handle it.

We worried so much about what might happen to Cayce if he got more involved in drugs. Later we found out from his friends and their parents that Cayce was always the designated driver. He was a role model for the others. When I learned this, I realized that I had probably overreacted. Years later, Cayce assured me that he had been telling the truth when he said the marijuana was for a friend.

After Cayce quit school and left home, he drifted along for a few weeks. He stayed with friends and worked part time. During this time, he reconciled with his father, went to visit him in Iowa, and stayed with him for several weeks.

Gradually Cayce began to get back on track. He came home and enrolled in an open campus school. He caught up in time to graduate on schedule, but open campus had no graduation ceremony. They mailed his diploma to him.

Although I fully accept the fact that I made a mistake in the way I handled the situation with Cayce, he believes he benefited from the experience. His choices put him in a position that helped him to mature.

Starting a new life

About three years into our marriage, Paul's brother, George, sent us a generous sum of money. He had been holding it in trust for Paul from their mother's estate. George had kept it for several years because he was afraid that Paul would spend it foolishly or that our marriage would end in divorce. He also wanted to be sure that we would use it wisely.

Although Paul was *not at all* interested in buying a home, I finally convinced him that we should. We looked at several houses and quickly found a ranch style home about fifteen miles east of Atlanta.

We used a large portion of the money from Paul's inheritance as a down payment on the house. The rest we used to pay debt. The layout of the house that we chose was perfect. It would provide privacy for us and Cayce could have two rooms on the opposite end of the home. We had hoped our getting into a new home would influence Cayce to move back in with us. Paul missed Cayce much more than I did. Cayce was adept at pushing my buttons. When he left home, I no longer had that aggravation to deal with. I discovered that I had finally reached the point where I no longer wished to participate in his games.

I was especially excited to move into our own home where we could have another dog. I had finally recovered from the grief of losing my Great Dane, Tim, in such a tragic way. I wanted another Dane and two weeks after we moved in, Duchess came to live with us. She was such a joy to us both.

Soon after we moved into our new house, Paul began to have considerable pain in his hip. The doctor told us that he would have to undergo radiation treatments. Paul began a series of treatments that completely exhausted him. Yet, as difficult as it was, he still managed to work five days a week!

His cancer had spread into his bones causing him almost unbearable pain. The doctors told us that they could probably end his pain, but the price he would have to pay would be high. It would almost surely mean moderate to complete loss of bladder and bowel functions. It was a difficult, but necessary, choice for him to make.

Paul was lucky. Only moderate bladder problems resulted, and he was completely pain free for several months. However, it took him several weeks to recover from the effects of radiation therapy.

I left my job shortly after Thanksgiving in 1987 and I didn't plan to seek other employment until after the first of the year.

Although I had no real interest, I looked at the classified ads daily just to see what was out there. One day, I saw two very simple ads. One simply stated Secretary Wanted and the other one was an ad for a CPT Operator.

I felt an overwhelming compulsion to follow up on these ads. I threw the newspaper in the trash at least six times before I finally called both numbers and made appointments.

The first interview for the secretarial position was at a firm that specialized in sports marketing. Secretarial work was *not* what I wanted. It made no sense to me why I just couldn't walk away. However, God was obviously leading me in that direction.

The owner of the firm interviewed me. He told me he was interested in my recent experience with typesetting. He asked me to call him in a month because of a project he had in the works. We both agreed I was not the right candidate for the secretarial job.

With relief, I headed for the next interview. They were looking for a word-processing operator to provide services for leased office suites. It was no great surprise to me when the manager hired me on the spot for part time work. She had discovered that finding a qualified CPT computer operator was almost impossible. I was an accomplished user with extensive programming skills as well, and that was exactly what she needed.

From the beginning, the manager told me that I should be in business for myself. She said that I was too smart and had too much on the ball to work for someone else. I told her I was too scared to be on my own. A couple of days later she tried a different approach. She gave me assignments that related to starting a business. One was to call and ask how to get a business license. Another time, she told me to find out how to register a company name. Then she told me to find out if a service business needed to establish tax accounts. Little by little, she was directing me to answers for all the questions I might have encountered about how to start my own business!

Meanwhile, a month had come and gone. When I called the first man who owned the agency that specialized in sports marketing, I learned he wasn't ready for my services. After I gave him my number, I tossed his card, never expecting to hear from him again. I assumed that since he was putting me off he was no longer interested. However, I did let him know how to reach me, *just in case*.

A couple of weeks later, I realized everything was practically in place to start my own business. I even suggested to my manager that perhaps I could start a small business right there in the office suites. If I continued to do their work part time along with my own, I could give them a percentage of my profits. She liked the idea, but said I must talk with the owner of the office suites and see if he would agree.

My supervisor and I were discussing the appointment I had made with the owner of the office suites. The phone rang and it was the man from the sports marketing agency. When I told him of my plan to meet with the owner of the office suites he immediately made me an unbelievable offer. He promised office space, furniture, business phone and a retainer if I would locate in his office. When I told him I must keep the other appointment first, he insisted I wait until my meeting with him to make a commitment.

This turn of events stunned me. They astonished my manager as well. As I was explaining to her what he had said to me, the phone rang again. It was the same man! "I'm serious!" he said.

Over the weekend, I thought about it and discussed it at length with my husband and parents. The following Monday I met with the owner of the office suites. He informed me that the only way they could consider something of that nature was to own it themselves and then hire me to run it. That would mean more security for me, but with all the progress I had made toward being a business owner, it was not what I was now looking for. When I told him of the other opportunity, he counseled me to take advantage of it. He told me that he really believed God was leading me to start my own business and he encouraged me to go for it.

In spite of my reluctance to give up a steady income from a dependable source, it was beginning to look like that was inevitable. Ever since I had begun to put God in the proper place in my life, positive things had been happening. Doors of opportunity opened for me. Wisely, I decided to follow God's leading.

In today's business atmosphere, handshake agreements are rare. The man who had offered me so much said a contract was *not* necessary, although if I wanted to draw up a legal paper it was okay with him. We both agreed that if a handshake were *not* enough, a contract would not be worth much either. Having made a verbal agreement, we shook hands. A week later, I was in business!

A few months after I started the typesetting business, my son, Paul, started his own picture framing business. Now we had even more in common. He was quite perceptive about running a business and I began to ask his advice on business matters.

The job that I had taken so reluctantly a couple of years earlier had, without my realizing it, prepared me to handle many aspects of a business on my own. There I gained a sampling of the skills I needed to begin my own business.

From the beginning, my typesetting business made a profit. It was a small profit, but enough to keep me going. I began to enjoy the freedom of being my own boss. The onset of my husband's pain, spreading cancer, and more radiation treatments overshadowed my enjoyment.

Cayce moved back in with us shortly after we bought the house and things went smoothly at first. However, he was the typical irresponsible teenager and it caused some problems between us when he didn't want to work. After a few months, he decided to join the service and left for boot camp. The day he got off the bus at camp, he fell on the ice and injured his back. Discharged without ever going through boot camp, he came home.

Cayce drifted from one job to the next and while working as a waiter at a local restaurant and bar, he met someone. He quickly became friends with her. He discovered that she had a little boy who was living with his grandmother in Tennessee. Cayce loved children and took every opportunity to be around them. His new girlfriend wanted to bring her son to Atlanta for a visit to celebrate his fifth birthday, but she had to work and didn't have a sitter. Cayce offered to baby-sit and fell in love with the child immediately. We all did! He was precious and precocious, and so polite.

Cayce brought the child to visit with us while he was babysitting him and we took them out to eat. We were celebrating my husband's birthday too. When we returned home, the boy climbed in my lap and told me he loved me. I too, fell in love that day.

Cayce took the boy back to his mother. He offered to drive them back to her mother's house in Tennessee. During the trip, the boy asked his mom if Cayce could be his new daddy. His mother didn't need much convincing and a couple of months later she and Cayce got married. The boy came to live with them and they all moved in with us. Paul and I both enjoyed having this extended family with us. They lived with us until September when they found a house about ten minutes from us. Although their leaving was difficult for us, it was a relief as well. It was time for them to be on their own. Paul and I needed to be alone. It was time for us to get serious about working on our own problems.

On a downhill slide

During the third year I was in business for myself, Cayce came to work with me. It was a busy year. We worked many late hours. Understanding that the clients had to come first was difficult for Paul. By now, I realized that it was imperative for the business to succeed. I needed security for the future. Paul, as usual, didn't want to consider my future without him! However, with twenty-eight years difference in our ages, and his failing health, I knew it was something that I had to consider.

Paul's insecurity and the fact that I had made my new business a priority caused a steady decline in our relationship. He couldn't function fully if I wasn't present and I couldn't function fully if I had to devote my entire attention to him.

We sought counseling and the therapist suggested divorce. I didn't want to hear it! I had come to love Paul in spite of his insecurities. Aware that his life was probably nearing the end, I was determined to stick it out, no matter what! I had come to realize that I was closer to Paul than I had ever been to any other man. I realized that, for the first time in my life, I really *did* know how to love someone.

For so many years, through all those relationships, divorce had been my solution. After the first divorce, subsequent divorces seemed much easier. I entered each successive relationship with the thought that there was an escape route. Now, with Paul, I found myself wanting to go the distance. I wanted to do what I could, within my own emotional limits, to help Paul finish his life and start his journey home. I didn't need someone encouraging me to quit. I already knew how to quit. Now I needed someone to show me how to finish.

I became progressively more uncomfortable with the therapist who had suggested divorce, so I began looking for a therapist who would be willing to help me make our marriage work. The therapist I found was a Christian counselor who understood my dilemma. She encouraged me to seek ways to focus on both my business and Paul. She helped me realize that I could still find time for myself by better scheduling. I came to realize that the major reason I was so miserable was that I had totally neglected time for myself. Consequently, I allowed more time for myself and my relationship with Paul improved.

Depending on Cayce to handle the office, I began taking time to nurture myself. This improved my spirits tremendously. My tolerance for my husband's neurotic needs grew.

As Paul's health rapidly deteriorated, he was on an emotional roller coaster. We decided to seek psychiatric help for him. He had become extremely depressed and more difficult to deal with than before. Subsequently, Paul spent a couple of weeks in a psychiatric hospital and went through intensive therapy for his depression. He seemed changed when he returned home. He was more secure and less demanding. I had hoped and prayed that things would change and miraculously, it seemed they had!

For several months, we enjoyed this new relationship. I now *wanted* to take off early from work and come home to him. For the first time in our married life, we were comfortable. As he became more enjoyable to be with, he became more of a priority to me. Cayce assumed some of my responsibilities at the office and I began to make a real marriage with Paul.

Much too soon this wonderful time of companionship ended. Paul began to experience severe pain and he started another course of radiation therapy. This was his third course of treatments in two years. His doctor told us the outcome would not be as positive this time. The effects were almost certain to be worse than before.

When I discussed Paul's situation with his older son, we mutually agreed that it was time for me to talk with the doctor. Late in January 1991, I called Paul's doctor and I asked about Paul's prognosis. My sixth sense had told me we were looking at a much shorter time than I wanted to think about. I told him Paul's son and I needed to know what to expect. We needed to make plans and prepare ourselves for the coming loss. The doctor told me that Paul had possibly three to six months left. It *could* be more, but he didn't think so.

Although we had been married more than seven years, we had enjoyed *only* five months of real happiness. We had finally begun to have a true marriage relationship, but sadly, we were nearing the end. I realized that I was going to have to be the one to tell him that he was dying. Both the doctor and Paul's son had agreed that it would be better for Paul if I were the one to break this terrible news to him. I prayed for courage and wisdom to know when and how to tell Paul. I asked God to give me words that would comfort us both. He did.

Paul and I went out to dinner a few nights later. As we sat in the restaurant, I knew in my heart that the time for telling was right then. I leaned in close to Paul. I told him that I had talked to his doctor. He seemed surprised. When I explained that we really needed to know what was coming so we could prepare ourselves, he wanted to know what the doctor had said. While I told him, we sat, holding hands. Tears were running down our cheeks as, oblivious to others in the noisy restaurant, we began our *long good-bye*. Life was going on all around us as if we were insignificant in the scheme of things. Yet, it was the most significant time of our life together.

Overall, Paul took the news very well. His recent psychiatric counseling had helped prepare him to cope with this devastating news. The doctor encouraged him to work for as long as he felt able. His employer was willing to go the distance. Paul was very close to the owner, the manager and several employees. None of them were ready to lose him either!

Earlier in the year, Cayce and his wife had told us they were pregnant. Paul was so happy. Thoughts of becoming a grandfather filled his mind with joy and pushed the cancer into the background. He began to focus on our eighth anniversary coming in September and the new baby who was due shortly after that. Paul was fighting to live to see both.

When Cayce's wife lost the baby, it devastated us. The loss affected Paul's will to survive; he gave up. He had lost hope for the future. Paul had been fighting to hang on for the baby's birth because it was so important to him. He wanted to be a grandfather and see his name carried into another generation. Now his reason to fight was gone!

Paul was going to be seventy-eight years old that April. As a diversion from what was happening, I began to focus on his birthday as a chance for him to say a formal "good-bye" to the many friends he loved.

I arranged to have an open house to celebrate his birthday and his life. I divided the day into three parts: fellow workers in the morning, friends in the early afternoon and family later in the day.

On the day of his birthday celebration, Paul was in his glory as he received his guests, played the host, clowned around with his walker and told jokes. The younger men he worked with were obviously sad. Paul worked doubly hard to cheer them up. For all of the guys at work, it was similar to losing a close relative. For two of them it was almost like losing a father!

Although it was a very tiring day, we got through it and the memories of that wonderful party filled Paul's mind in the following weeks.

Paul continued to work shorter hours. He brought the work home. In early May, he stopped going out to work. His employer began to bring the work to our home.

Because we were very concerned that our dog might accidentally cause Paul to fall, we reluctantly sent Duchess to stay with Cayce for the last few weeks of Paul's life. We brought her home briefly for Paul to say "good-bye" to her a few days before he died.

As the end rapidly approached, Paul and I began to talk about his death. Our anger surprised us both when it rose to the surface. One night, he was being unusually obnoxious to me. I went into the other room to read the paper. I refused to go to him when he called out to me.

After a little while, when I had regained my composure I went back to him. I sat on the bed while I apologized. I said, *"I was so mad at you!"* then *"I'm mad because you're leaving me!"* I started crying and he did too.

Paul said, "I'm mad because you're staying. I want you to come with me! *I'm afraid to go alone!"*

It literally tore my heart out. I did *not* want him to have to make this journey alone. Yet it's something we all have to face. I reminded him that God would be there to guide him through everything. Again, God gave me the right words. They seemed to calm Paul's fears and he moved forward with newly found courage from that point.

Paul began sharing every feeling and thought, despite how painful. We stopped lashing out at each other. It was a beautiful, though sorrowful time.

Almost two weeks later, I observed as Paul became confused while speaking with a client over the telephone. I gently took the phone from him and explained to the client what was happening. I put Paul to bed.

I told him that he needed his energy to sustain him through the days ahead. He began to babble incoherently. He no longer comprehended what was happening.

The end was closing in on us. We still needed to do so much. Paul's son and daughter-in-law came to stay with us. He is a Rabbi and she is a therapist who specializes in helping terminally ill patients deal with death and dying. She worked with Paul daily, helping him to prepare for his passing, while the closest members of the family hovered nearby.

Cayce ran the office so that I could be home with Paul the last two weeks. After he closed the office, Cayce would come and bunk on the floor next to his dad. It was a precious time of closeness for all of us.

Years later, though, Cayce told me how much he had sacrificed for me to be with Paul those last days. He had needed to be there too. He just couldn't tell me. He believed I needed him in the office and he shouldered that responsibility without question.

Cayce later told me that it helped him to understand how I felt when my grandmother died. He is still struggling to come to terms with not being able to *be* with his dad as much as he needed to those last two weeks. If he had only spoken up, we might have found a way to meet his needs *and* those of the business.

In spite of all the counseling, at the end, letting go was hard for Paul. The end was eminent and our daughter-in-law told us all to withdraw and return to work. Paul would have no alternative but to let go. We believed the reason he was fighting so hard was to make it to the first of the month so I'd have another social security check. He was suffering terribly! It needed to end!

Hospice was involved for the last month of Paul's life. They were doing all they could to alleviate his pain, but it wasn't enough. Every time I

On a downhill slide

spoke to Paul, he would rally. Gradually, because of my daughter-in-law's advice, everyone withdrew from him. They said their "good-byes" and then did not speak to him again although they continued to help me tend his physical needs.

His son and daughter-in-law were next to the last to say "good-bye." She encouraged him to let go and stop suffering. Then they left him to visit a local monastery. A friend from our church came to sit with Paul so I could return to my office. It was extremely difficult for me to leave, but I told him that I had to go back to work. Nothing was pressing at the office, but our daughter-in-law told me that Paul would continue to fight. She said he would linger and suffer until I left. Therefore, with a heavy heart, I told Paul "good-bye" and went to my office.

It happened just the way my daughter-in-law said it would. Almost immediately, after I got to the office, I received a call from my friend saying that Paul had died. I was numb with grief as I realized that he was gone. In spite of the counsel I'd received from our daughter-in-law, I was angry with her. I felt guilty and angry with myself because I was not at his side when he died.

Somehow, we all made it through that Memorial Day weekend. Friends and family gave up their holiday to mourn and bury Paul. The boys and I turned it into a time of drawing together. We remembered all the fun and laughter Paul had brought into our lives. They had all called him "Pops." In many ways, he was more of a father figure to my older sons than their own father had been. It was a sad time for them.

When we first met, Paul kept a mannequin's hand that he would hide in the most unusual places. When discovered, it always caused us to laugh! Paul took it to the grocery store and used it to hand over the cash or credit card! I found it under my pillow, in my jewelry box or among the towels. When I finally tired of the joke, he gave the hand away. We rarely spoke of it afterward. A couple of weeks before he died, he told me he wanted his son to get a mannequin's hand to put in the casket with him. He wanted us to place it in a conspicuous place to make people laugh. I mentioned it to my stepson, but he failed to follow through.

At the cemetery, the workers began filling the grave. We looked up and, first one, then another started laughing, as it registered with all of us. Within minutes, everyone had joined in! Paul's grave was just across from a "praying hands" statue! Paul had gotten his last wish after all! We were laughing! As melancholy as Paul's whole life had been, he had always made others laugh. At his grave, the laughter swept over us as we remembered his capricious humor! Then we understood. We would still be laughing at his jokes and celebrating our time with him for years to come. True to his nature, Paul had the last laugh!

Is anyone there?

When there is a death in the family, everyone draws closer together. Have you ever noticed that when the funeral is over, everyone goes their separate ways, leaving those closest to the loss to mourn alone?

That's just what happened in my case. Family and friends filled Paul's last days. Then when the funeral was over everyone disappeared. I was alone as I faced the future without Paul.

I needed to get away. I needed to distance myself while I contemplated the future. I took a five-day cruise to be alone. Having been on several cruises before with Paul, I knew how to achieve the isolation I needed without being completely by myself as I would have been at home. Socializing only at meals, I walked the decks or sat and stared at the water as I continued the grieving process. When I returned home, I was in better shape emotionally. Yet, I wasn't yet prepared to face the reality of a life alone.

After Paul's death, Mark stood by me the longest. The others, both family and friends, seemed to evaporate from my life. It was an incredibly lonely time of adjustment for me.

Cayce left the business. At his wife's urging, they moved to Tennessee. This not only upset my life on a personal level, it devastated my business.

In my heart, I knew it was time for Cayce to cut the apron strings completely. Still, losing him at this crucial time was hard. Because we worked so closely together in the business, I had come to depend on him more than ever.

Months later, I discovered that the primary reason for their move was to resolve serious problems in their marriage. His wife believed those problems were the result of Cayce's relationship with me.

It was months before they initiated contact with me. I wisely allowed them their space, however, their absence added a new dimension to my feelings of loss.

Paul's death left me in a precarious financial situation. I had lost his salary and social security income. He had no life insurance. I knew that my brother-in-law wouldn't send money indefinitely, and I didn't want him to feel responsible for me.

The emotional pain clouded everything I tried to do. Deciding my future was difficult. Fortunately, I realized that, without some kind of emotional support, I might slip back into the old destructive patterns.

I had no intimate friends. No one was there for me to talk to except Mark. No one was *there* for me while I worked through grief over losing my husband and the security he provided.

I wanted to go to church; I needed to go. However, each time I went I experienced my loss more intensely. I felt as if I would smother to death and I could *not* hold back the tears. People would come up to me and say comforting things, then walk away. They disappeared from my life until the next time I saw them in church. What I really needed was for someone to take my arm and say, "Come home with us for lunch today. You can stay and visit if you like. If you don't have time to stay, just eat and run. We just want to be with you."

Instead, they said, "We'll have you over real soon." In the following weeks those invitations never materialized. I was lonelier than ever.

Because of this experience, I never generalize an invitation. If I can't make it specific, I keep quiet. It's too easy to walk away and never follow up. Perhaps I expected too much from others, but I really needed something I didn't get from those I considered friends, my family or the church.

Not finding what I needed elsewhere, I turned to others to ease my grief. I joined an AARP therapy group for widows and widowers and attended several meetings. They suggested ballroom dancing as an acceptable way to reenter the social scene. They easily convinced me. I knew firsthand that dancing made me feel good. Dancing was something I really enjoyed, but it had taken me into the wrong atmosphere in times past. Remembering that, I promised myself that I would *not* make the same mistakes again.

I decided to start at a dance studio. I wanted to learn to waltz and do the rumba. However, I didn't want to go back into the Latin clubs. I was afraid that it would point me down the wrong path again. I didn't have the money to pay for lessons, so I took the introductory course to brush up.

I wasn't interested in looking for another companion. I just wanted to be around people who were having a good time. I began going to ballroom dances to socialize with others. Right away, I met a friendly group of people who went from club to club to dance. They didn't drink or smoke. They were interesting and being with them was fun. They immediately accepted me into their group and treated me as if I *really was* important to them. For the first time, I had a group of social friends. Moreover, I was enjoying dancing with some of the best dancers in town!

These new friends called me during the week just to chat or to check on me. Several of them had lost their life's partners as well. Many of them knew what I was going through. They actively sought my company. They encouraged me as I began to face the future *alone*. We tend to go where we know we're wanted and appreciated. That's where I went: dancing with my friends.

In late August 1991, Daddy suffered several brain strokes. Diagnosed with Alzheimer's, Mother placed him in a nursing home against my wishes. I wanted to bring him to my home to care for him. Everyone said it would be too hard. It might have been. However, I will never know for sure. My mother decided to put him in the nursing home because she felt it was her only choice. It took a long time for me to process the sadness over that situation. I was angry with my mother because she did *not* allow me the opportunity to care for my daddy.

I found it difficult to deal with the terrible conditions Daddy endured in the nursing facility. Daddy's roommate hit him several times.

It was several months before we could get daddy into a private room. The aides did not keep him as clean as we would have liked. The stench of urine was everywhere. Roaches sometimes got on the beds and once, I saw them on the tray of food they brought my daddy. It was unthinkable that he had to be in such a place!

Once, Mark observed an attendant using physical force against Daddy. I felt powerless to do anything about the situation. I decided that if I could physically manage, none of my loved ones would ever suffer that kind of fate again! Not even my mother, with whom I was still very angry!

After Paul's death, none of my sons had attempted to include me in their lives. It didn't upset me, because I had no desire to be involved extensively in their lives. Consequently, I surprised them when I told them I had met someone and that I was again contemplating marriage.

One evening in October, I was out dancing and an older man came up to me and asked me to dance. He introduced himself as Jerry.

The moment Jerry took me in his arms, I breathed a prayer, "Lord, please don't ever let this man leave me! I want to dance with him forever!" The firm yet respectful way he held me made me feel so safe and secure. He was such a smooth dancer that we practically floated around the dance floor.

When he escorted me back to my table, Jerry didn't ask if he could join me. He just sat! Later, as I became acquainted with him, I realized that this was totally out of character for him. I asked him about it and he replied, "I was afraid to ask. You might have said no, so I just staked my claim."

Jerry had been a widower for several years. He had taken an early retirement to nurse his wife through her struggle with emphysema. I could see right away that he knew about *real* commitment.

Jerry quickly became the center of my life. We went dancing. We went to the mountains. We had a good time, no matter what we were doing. While in the mountains, we were driving along and looking at the sights when I saw a cute wedding chapel. I didn't realize what it was until I had already pointed it out to Jerry. "Let's get married," Jerry said.

His remark was unexpected. It upset me so much that I started crying. It was too soon after Paul's death. It was too soon in this new relationship to have to tell him my marital history. However, because of what he had just said, I knew I had to tell him right then before things got out of hand. If Jerry were still interested after hearing all the details, then it might be worth the risk of becoming involved with him.

When I finished telling him, Jerry told me that nothing in the past mattered. He said he truly regretted the pain and sorrow I had experienced over the years. He then told me that it did *not* change the way he already felt toward me. It didn't lessen his respect for me, and he continued to treat me like a princess.

A few weeks later, I had foot surgery. Jerry moved into my spare room so that he could drive me everywhere I needed to go. He had been living with his daughter about an hour's drive away. Thanks to Jerry, I could continue working.

As Christmas approached, I gradually became aware that Jerry was getting very serious. It was nothing he said. He just began to act increasingly like a loving husband. My friends began to tell me they thought he was going to *pop the question* any day. I was hoping he wouldn't. I was *not* ready to say yes and I *did not* want to put him off. I was afraid it might drive him away.

We went shopping for a jewelry-cleaning machine. We headed for a particular store, but on our way, he wanted to stop at the mall. Once there, Jerry steered me into every jewelry store. I could tell what he had on his mind, and I tried to stay aloof as I looked at everything except engagement rings. We finally made it to Service Merchandise. When we got to the jewelry counter, he began actively encouraging me to look at engagement rings.

Although I tried on several rings, I was still not ready to say yes. After a half hour of looking at first one and then another, Jerry asked me which one I liked. Reluctantly I told him. The clerk asked me when the big day was going to be. I laughed nervously. I told him that as far as I knew, there wasn't going to be a big day. I hadn't received a proposal!

Immediately, with a huge smile, Jerry asked me to be his wife. He had instinctively chosen the right time and the right place. My heart melted, and I heard myself say, "Yes!"

I told Jerry I wasn't emotionally ready for marriage so soon. I needed more time. He understood completely. He was supportive as I continued to grieve for Paul. Besides the grief over Paul's death, I was now dealing with the futile battle my father was fighting. He was slowly losing his sanity and I felt as if I were losing my grip as well. Jerry understood what I was going through. He continued to support and comfort me as I cried my way through our engagement.

At first, only Cayce approved of our marriage. The others let me know that they would prefer me to remain single. I told them that I could understand their objections, but I had found someone special. It was up to me to decide whether to be lonely or happy in a secure marriage.

It wasn't like with some families. They showed no anger toward either of us. However, it was a couple of years before they realized I had been right. They had to see for themselves that I was happy and that Jerry was treating me well. Once they saw how he treated my mother, daddy, *and* Aunt Edris, they loved him too. My sons had been worried that I could possibly soon suffer another loss since Jerry was twenty-one years older than I. They had wanted to protect themselves and me from more grief.

With only Jerry's family firmly in approval of our marriage, I began a new chapter in life. My life was full of love, devotion and an abundance of affection. I had it all! Marriage to Jerry was the best decision I had ever made.

There were still a few important things to discuss. I broached the subject of religion and the possibility that I would ultimately become responsible for my parents and Aunt Edris. Jerry had been raised Catholic but did not attend religious services. However, he assured me that he would never interfere with my church attendance. He also vowed to stand by me as I honored my responsibilities to my family.

The Bible admonishes Christians against being "unequally yoked." However, I completely disregarded that sound advice and married anyway. I based my decision entirely on Jerry's solemn word that my religious faith and family responsibilities would never be an issue.

In March, we welcomed a new grandson. Paul and his wife had a little boy. Tempering the joy of his arrival was the fact that my late husband, Paul, had so wanted another grandchild in the family but was not here to enjoy it.

Our delightful grandson turned out to be a real live wire, never staying still. He brought such joy to our family.

My heart didn't know which emotion to feel! Should I be angry and sad over Daddy's decline? Should I give in to my grief for Paul? Should I be happy about my engagement? Was it proper that feelings for my new companion or joy for a new grandchild override all the other feelings?

Through it all, Jerry stood by me and helped give purpose and meaning to my life. We began planning for our wedding in May. Even then, I had not yet realized that I had met the "love of my life." I had been searching for Jerry! I just didn't know it! That is quite evident when you read the next two poems.

We took our vows in front of our immediate families and a few close friends. A week later, we went on a cruise. A major depression overshadowed our honeymoon, although I did my best to hide it from Jerry. I didn't want to spoil our special time together. We came home from our cruise, and as we left the airport, Jerry suggested we buy flowers for me to put on Paul's grave. We did. Jerry sat in the car as I told Paul about the happiness I had found. I told Paul that he would always occupy a special place in my heart. I assured him that my heart was big enough for both of them.

We left the cemetery and went home to start our new life together. Although it didn't happen immediately, the pain of loss began to subside as life went on. Jerry understood that I had *not* completed the grieving process. He stood by me patiently as I continued to process my grief.

Thoughts of love

I always knew…sometime…someplace
There had to be a face…picked out of the crowd,
To look at…to love…to cherish…
To wish that…somehow…someday…
There would be a way that I would come to know
The thoughts…the dreams…the hopes…the schemes…
That lay beneath that beloved face…
And, to feel…to share…to love…to be there
To soothe and help with life's many cares.
My Darling, these were my hopes…my deepest desires…
With the magic of you my soul's now on fire.
Ablaze with the warmth of passion and love
My spirit now soaring like a dove…
Fulfilled in knowing that you are my love.

A note to the one I love

This is not a new experience, this love I feel for
you. It is ageless, timeless. It has always existed;
or seems to have been in my heart, my very being.
For I have loved the very essence of you
for as long as I can remember.
I have searched for you in everyone I met
but found only fragments;
tiny, teasing threads of you that made me sure
that somewhere the whole and complete YOU
really did exist.
And, if I waited patiently and long enough,
you would come to me. And you did!

Don't forget the little things

In the hustle and bustle and whirl of the day,
Caught up in oneself, living life YOUR own way
Not making that phone call or dropping a line
To let those you LOVE know they're still on your mind.
With loved ones forgotten: and friends far away,
Facing problems ALONE with the chores of the day;
Not LIVING your life—you're just drifting along.
And all the time wondering: WHAT went wrong?

Imagine your life and your world years from now,
Without your life's work—or sweat on your brow
With NOTHING to do and time standing still,
And THINK of the void in YOUR life you could fill
With family and friends and things to DO,
If you'd only kept UP with the loved ones you knew,
And friends who were there—but are now hard to find
'Cause you failed to nurture the ties that bind.

If you DON'T 'seize the day', put your problems at bay
When you're old, past your prime, at the END of your way
Your phone will be silent—your mail: junk and bills
With NONE to console you while climbing life's hills.
So, call that dear friend, let them know you'll be there.
Tell them YOU love them and really DO care.
For the gesture made NOW that nurtures THEIR soul
May someday return and make YOUR life whole.

Julie

Oh Julie, Dear Julie, our sweet baby girl,
You've come to our family, our hearts are awhirl.
With love and emotion, it's hard to express
This feeling you've brought us—it's true happiness!

Oh Julie, Sweet Julie, our hearts overflow
With love and devotion. We all love you so.
Oh Julie, Dear Julie, our sweet little girl,
Oh Julie, Sweet Julie—We're glad you're OUR GIRL!

Oh Julie, Dear Julie, you're simply great.
Oh Julie, Sweet Julie, 'twas well worth the wait.
It seemed such a long time, but now here you are;
Oh Julie, Sweet Julie—you're our shining star!

Oh Julie, Sweet Julie, our hearts overflow
With love and devotion. We all love you so.
Oh Julie, Dear Julie, our sweet little girl,
Oh Julie, Sweet Julie—We're glad you're OUR GIRL!

The Lord giveth and the Lord taketh away!

Before our wedding, I had only seen Cayce and his wife a couple of times after they moved to Tennessee. They were pregnant again. They began to draw closer to us. We eagerly anticipated the birth of their new baby.

Business had declined drastically over the past year. In May, I decided to move my business into my home. I wasn't sure if God was telling me it was time to do something else, so I decided to pray about it. God led me to set up at home as if I were already in business. If I received no work during the first month, I planned to close the business and look for a job. Within two days after getting my new business phone, I had two calls and I was in business!

In September 1992, my first granddaughter was born. In celebration of her birth, I wrote a song for her. The melody is like the tinkling sound of a music box.

In October, I spent a couple of days in the hospital for minor surgery that resulted in a massive infection and a second hospital stay for a week.

Three weeks after I got out of the hospital, Daddy got sick with pneumonia. The nursing home sent him to the hospital. We all knew he would never get well. Because of Alzheimer's the doctor told us that he would never again eat without taking food into his lungs, which would in turn cause pneumonia. A feeding tube was the only alternative. My daddy had expressed his final wishes long before and we knew it was time to implement them.

Even in my weakened condition, I was emotionally stronger than my mother. Thus, she left it up to me to decide. The torch had finally passed to my generation. After consulting with the doctors, I accepted the fact that my daddy was dying. My daddy did *not* want heroic measures taken on his behalf. Therefore, I asked the doctors to make him comfortable, but to do nothing to prolong his life. The doctors encouraged me in this decision.

We arranged for hospice to help us through the next phase and brought him to our home to die. He died a week later.

The night it happened, I was restless and could not sleep. I walked back and forth from our bedroom to where my parents were sleeping. Finally, I lay down on the floor between the two beds. A few minutes later, as I got up to check on Daddy, I accidentally knocked against Mother's bed and she woke up. She also decided to get up and check on Daddy. We were both telling him how much we loved him and patting his arm as he breathed his last breath seconds later. I believe God caused my restlessness thus permitting both of us to be right there when my daddy needed us most.

In the midst of my grief, in an attempt to process the pain I was feeling, I wrote a poem. It appeared in the July/August 1995 issue of *Bereavement Magazine*. The poem later became the basis of a country/western song that I wrote entitled "Master Plan."

If my daddy could have spoken

If my daddy could have spoken,
He'd have said these words I know.
He always tried to comfort us
Because he loved us so.

I can almost hear him as he speaks
These words of comfort dear.
It moves my soul—it heals my heart;
Now listen—can you hear?

"I wandered far from home today;
I left you all behind.
Your loving faces, by my side,
Drift slowly through my mind.

'Twas not an easy thing to do,
And yet I could not stay.
I feel so torn, so bruised and sad
But, I must go my way.

There comes a time in all our lives
When we must say "good-bye."
For me, this is that time in life
It's now my time to die.

But, loved ones—do not mourn me,
For I lived my life full well.
And spent my time preparing
For the place where I will dwell.

And surely you must know how much
You all have meant to me;
But through these last hard days—you've
Shown your depth of love for me.

Now remember life's for living;
Don't let sorrow get you down.
Face the challenge of tomorrow
With a smile and not a frown.

And remember when it's over
We'll be together once again.
Just hold on to God's sweet promise
For He has a *Master Plan!*"

Master Plan

It was a cold November morning
When my daddy went away.
Mama whispered "Please don't leave me"
As she knelt where Daddy lay.

"You know we can't go on without you
This will be life's hardest test."
But my daddy didn't hear her
'Cause by now he was at rest."

The day before my daddy died,
He said some real important things
"Child, be good to your sweet mama now
Give her my wedding ring."

"You'll have to help Mama raise the younger kids
And I wish you lots of luck
Give Uncle Joe dad's old shotgun
And you can have my pickup truck."

Then my Daddy said…

"I hadn't planned to leave so soon.
And I really didn't want to go.
I see you crying by my side,
Don't you know I love you so?"

"But, remember my dear loved ones
We'll be together once again.
Just hold on to God's sweet promise
For He has a *Master Plan!*"

It was a rainy April morning
When my mama passed away
As she lay there in her big old bed
I heard her softly say:

"Child, your daddy never lied to us
When he spoke of God's own plan.
Just hold on to that sweet promise
Till we see you once again."

Just hold on to God's sweet promise
For He has a *Master Plan!*

A wedding, a funeral and more

After Daddy died, Mother's health and mental abilities quickly deteriorated. I was certain that she had Alzheimer's too. Her doctor confirmed our suspicions a few months later. It was just a matter of time before we would need to make special care arrangements for her as well. I had no idea just how complicated and serious life was about to become. Everything I had gone through until now had just been a shadow of what was to be!

Somehow, we got through 1993. It was a blur. I worked hard. I cried often. I slept too much. I tried not to forget the happiness of my new marriage.

The major traumatic events that year were a decline of my business and emergency laser surgery on my right eye in April. The surgery repaired my eye but left a permanent vision problem.

In January 1994, Stephen called to tell me he was getting married in less than four weeks. He needed my assistance to pull it together. I designed and sent invitations, typeset a wedding program, recorded all the music and even found time to buy a new dress!

In the midst of it all, Paul called me to tell me that David, my first husband, would be at the wedding. He also told me that his father was gravely ill. Paul said he wanted to tell me more but was not at liberty to do so.

In February, at the last minute, I had to fly to Stephen's wedding because of an ice storm. We weren't sure if we could get there by car if we waited, so I went on ahead. As it turned out, Jerry made it safely.

The power was off until about a half hour before the service. I had prepared candles for a candlelight service, but the cold was difficult to deal with. Two kerosene heaters were set up and that helped. The carpet in the sanctuary had been soaked because of a leak. We all got wet feet. Then, we all got a scare when the bride was late getting to the church! We were afraid she had been in an accident.

Added to that strain, was the stress of coming face to face with my ex-husband and seeing how sick he looked. I wouldn't have recognized David on the street.

Kenn was there as the wedding photographer. Stephen and his bride had forgotten to arrange for ushers, so Jerry became an usher. It may have seemed a little strange to outsiders if they had known the relationship of those who attended. However, we accepted it as normal. Everyone was not only civilized, we were friendly! Stephen had invited Marco as well, but he was unable to make the trip.

Jerry again proved his trust and the depth of his love for me. He encouraged me to sit with David at the reception so we could talk things out and make our peace.

The wedding was the catalyst needed for the healing process to begin for the two of us. Through the years, the boys had suffered because they had to choose between us for family affairs. David had refused to occupy the same room with me. He was now willing to have a family portrait made and he took all of us to dinner after the reception.

As the family balance shifted, it confounded Paul. He found it difficult to comprehend. He had walked a tightrope between us for so long. It was several months before he could adjust to our new relationship. He believed the truce was tenuous at best. He kept expecting something to happen to change things back to the way they had been for so many years.

Life isn't always fair

Life just isn't fair; nor is it ever likely to be. There will always be those who have more or are stronger. The grass will always look greener on the other side of the fence. Far better to learn this now instead of later and to be willing to adapt and cope with setbacks and disappointments instead of focusing only on your needs and wants, thus, making your life bitter with unreasonable expectations.

David, the Poet
used with permission

Endurance

Those who stick it out to the very end no matter the cost resisting the temptation and urges to play the field are to be praised, respected and admired for their endurance, for they have learned to overcome adversity instead of being ruled by the baser qualities of anger, pride and hate.

These are the very ones, who, having paid the highest price know what the meaning of love is and how to truly love.

David, the Poet
used with permission

Invalidation

When you tell me all the reasons why I should *not* feel the way I do, you invalidate my feelings. The feelings I have may not be appropriate, but they are painfully real to me.

Color-blind

What lies hidden in the heart is what really matters...Not the color that covers one from head to toe.

David, the Poet
used with permission

An open letter to my sons

Shortly after Stephen's wedding, I wrote a letter to my sons:

To my dear children,

I want to say so much. Knowing where to begin is hard for me.

I had never come to terms with myself over my divorce from your father until over the last week. Feelings began to surface when I realized your daddy and I would both be attending Stephen's wedding. After the wonderful, healing experience of that evening—even more feelings surfaced.

When I saw your dad, so obviously sick, my heart was completely broken. I regretted the years we had both wasted and the pain we caused our children and each other. My heart softened enough that God could deal with *me*. I was finally able to face the truth about the role I had played in our marriage. Because of my own pain, I had buried everything deeply within myself. I always encouraged you to have an open mind and open heart toward your dad. I encouraged each of you to pursue a relationship with him. Even so, dealing with the facts of what I had done to my family was impossible for me. Every time I came close to dealing with it, the pain would be so intense that I had to back away. I shoved it deeper and deeper. I hid myself in relationships that could generate enough "stuff" for me to deal with to keep the past deeply buried within me.

For many years, I couldn't acknowledge that the role I played strongly influenced the breakup of our home. Saying, "If only he hadn't done this, I wouldn't have done that," was easy. However, it isn't quite that simple. Each of us must take responsibility for our own actions instead of projecting the blame on circumstances or each other.

During the wedding service, the pastor admonished Stephen and his bride not to allow a third party to gain admittance to their problems unless it was Christ. He told them to walk through life hand-in-hand until "one should lay the other to rest in the arms of Jesus." Those words touched me deeply. I wish I had been receptive to such a message as I began my life with your dad.

Your daddy and I were very young when we married. We were too immature to handle the responsibilities of marriage. Of the two of us, I was the least mature. I was ill prepared—physically and emotionally, to make the kind of commitment a successful marriage requires. I didn't know enough. I was naïve. I had no idea what marriage was all about. That was the first strike against us. In addition, I married to get away from home rather than for love. I *did* love your dad, and still do. However, it was *not* the mature love necessary to build a solid marriage foundation.

Your dad came from a broken home with no father figure to guide him. That was the second strike against us.

We didn't know the three-step process necessary to problem solving: 1) "identify the problem, 2) propose a solution, and 3) implement the solution." Then, move on! Like many others, we kept on identifying the problem. If one of us proposed a solution, we never followed through. We reverted to identifying the problem. It was an endless circle of frustration that got us nowhere.

Now I think of my immaturity as stupidity, selfishness and insensitivity. I could *not* handle the responsibilities and the close relationship of two such different people.

An open letter to my sons

Since I saw your dad, I have realized that in order for the healing to be complete, I had to acknowledge my part in the failure of our marriage. I must finally deal with this painful truth and put it behind me. Of all that I have done in my life, most of which you already know about, I am most ashamed of one thing. It was emotional cruelty at its worst. I can't imagine how it must have hurt him. Just thinking about how he suffered because of my careless words made me ashamed and remorseful. You see, I told your dad that I didn't love him, never had, and probably never would. I told him that I had always loved someone else. To make matters even worse, we became best friends with that person and his wife. Although I didn't act on those feelings for the other person, the closeness of the relationship subjected both of us to unbelievable pain and stress.

Perhaps, if we had *not* wasted so much of our energy on pursuing that relationship, we might have saved our marriage. Instead, we left the legacy of our fractured family to our daughters-in-law and grandchildren.

To say that I was confused during that time of our lives would be an understatement. I was in my forties before I realized that *love* doesn't hurt someone else. Only selfishness and self-centeredness do that!

Although our childhood and the way our parents raised us set the stage for this disaster, *we* played the major roles. Under the circumstances *we* created for ourselves, neither of us had a chance to grow up. We were unable to deal with each other's problems, much less our own.

Essentially, we were dysfunctional before we got married. Marriage only exacerbated the problem.

And now, for you—Cayce,

When your father and I got married, we had a little more going for us. Although he was quite young, he loved your older brothers. He interacted with them in a beautiful way. Our relationship had much potential, but again, I wasn't ready for all the pressures and problems that often beset a young family. As it turned out, neither was he.

We did fine, except financially, until we moved out west for my health. Your dad was wonderful when I was sick. He encouraged me to do what was necessary to get well. He was willing to move to the other side of the country to accomplish that goal.

After we moved to Phoenix, we couldn't find jobs. Our money was running out, and we were beginning to get desperate. We tried any way we could to make a few dollars. At first, we stayed in church and depended on God to see us through. Although God did His part, like Eve, I failed my test. My failure set the stage for your father to fail as well.

The day came when I finally broke. I became so depressed that I thought I couldn't go on. I wrote a note to that effect and left it on the kitchen counter. I felt relieved for having dumped my negativity on paper and I went back to work and made a big sale.

I was so excited; I rushed home to share the news with everyone. When I got there, I found the yard swarming with police officers. Your dad had come home and found my note. Because of my past, he had interpreted it as a suicide note. That incident upset him so much that he decided to leave the church. He got a job in a nightclub to support us and when he walked away from church, I followed.

Leaving the church set us both up for all the temptations of the world. Instead of solving our problems, it added to them immeasurably.

We went out into the world of dancing, drinking and all that goes with it. We embraced the popular idea of the day that free love was the way to happiness. We had entered the era of open marriage, instant gratification and disposable children.

An open letter to my sons

We neglected you, our children. We left you to take care of each other while we went out and worked the nightclubs for the photography business. As we partied, we grew apart. Infidelity became my drug of choice to deaden the pain of a dying marriage. I won't try to excuse or justify anything I did in that era of my life because justification is impossible.

When your dad and I ended our marriage, I thought my life was over. I had lost my self-respect. How could I expect anyone else to respect me? I set about to find relationships that would provide the punishment I deserved. In other words, I tried to destroy myself. In my selfishness and self-centered behavior, and to my eternal regret and sorrow, I didn't consider what the consequences would be to my children.

It was not until I met Marcus and Wendy that I began to outgrow my compulsive self-destructive behavior. They helped me so much by telling me I was strong to have survived, not weak for having succumbed. It was the defining moment.

Then Marco came along and encouraged me to go back to church and to be reconciled with my parents. He was addicted to tranquilizers and drank a lot, but he had a good heart. We needed each other to break out of our destructive cycles. He and I believe we saved each other's lives, but circumstances doomed our marriage from the start. Added to the substance abuse on his part, and emotional instability on mine, too many cultural differences existed. Dealing with you and Paul was difficult for him. He didn't want to be a stepfather. He wanted to be your friend. However, you needed a father figure more. In the end, he couldn't overcome his own problems and deal with the family pressures simultaneously. He chose to save himself and walked away.

However, because of the tremendous growth during that relationship, I was finally ready to live as a single mother. Our life as a family began coming together. It wasn't until I had reached this point in my life that

I was ready for a "till death do us part" relationship. When "Pops" came into our lives, we became a real family. By this time, you were ready to grow up and move away from the family. Although Pops was good for all of us, it would have been better if he had appeared earlier in your life.

Now, for all of you: It was bad enough that we nearly destroyed ourselves. However, knowing the pain and sorrow we caused each of you is the greatest burden I have to bear. All of you have been wonderfully forgiving. However, I'm sure I will never comprehend the depth of emotional pain I caused you to suffer.

I can only tell you, as I told David, that I apologize. I am sorry for any hurt, pain, sorrow, and unhappiness that you have endured because of my mistakes. Please take comfort in the knowledge that none of it was intentional. I know that doesn't erase the consequences, and it does *not* negate the pain, but it is *all* I have to offer.

We cannot go back. We can only go forward one day at a time. I know I can never totally repair the damage I did to your fathers or to each of you. That is a burden I will carry to my grave.

My dear, dear children, I have always loved you. Unfortunately, I didn't know how to be a good wife, and that set the stage for me to be an inadequate mother as well. Please forgive me.

Love, Mom

If one good thing leads to another, it's okay to feel good about yourself!

Be as *Good*—as good as you can be.
Do some *Good*—for everyone you see.
And make *Good* on all you say you'll do,
Even when no one is watching you.

Seek out *Good*—in everyone you meet.
Find some *Good*—in those you greet.
Speak of *Good* and that is all,
And you'll *Feel Good*—as you stand tall.

Yes, head and shoulders above the rest,
For you have passed life's hardest test.
You've passed it well, for all to see
Just how *Good* someone can be.

And, just how *Good* can someone be?
As *Good* as they decide to be!
So, listen well and hear me out.
The choice is yours, without a doubt.

It's *Good or Bad*—just black or white.
No grays allowed—just what is right.
So, choose you, now, and choose you well.
Make life on earth like Heaven—not Hell.

Think twice!

Don't lose yourself in the insanity of "doing the same thing over and over while expecting different results."

Don't make the mistake of carrying hatred in your heart. It is the equivalent of trying to kill the one you hate by taking the poison yourself!

The healing continues

The following month, Paul's in-laws scheduled a birthday party for our grandson at their home. Before the reconciliation, Paul would have invited only one of us to attend. This time, David and I both went to our grandson's party. We spent time together healing the old wounds. I asked David if he would like to come to our house for Mark's birthday party in April. He said he would love to come.

When David came to the party, we could tell he had gotten much worse. He had not given up hope, but he still didn't talk about it to us. David came early and stayed late. He couldn't seem to tear himself away from the family. I didn't want it to end either. I was beginning to see a little of the man I had once loved. The healing of our pain was so powerful, we were reluctant to let it end.

I had planned a birthday party for two of our daughters-in-law in August. As he left, David promised to come.

In June, Jerry underwent prostate surgery with a good outcome. The doctor's test didn't detect cancer and he recovered in record time. As he was recovering, Mark's wife had major surgery and came to stay with us to recuperate.

I had previously offered to help Aunt Edris clear away the remnants of a lifetime and organize her affairs. In July, she decided it was time. I spent Wednesdays and Saturdays working toward that end. It was an hour's drive each way, so it made for some very tiring days.

By now, my mother had been in the hospital twice within four months and she continued to decline. We began to think about what was to come. Meanwhile, Aunt Edris, who lived next door to my mother, became incapacitated. She was losing her sight due to cataracts. She was an insulin-dependent diabetic. She had developed postural hypotension and could only be on her feet for a few minutes at a time. She had previously undergone surgery for cancer, had suffered a minor stroke, and had a major heart attack. Now, she no longer could drive or properly care for herself.

In early August, I received word that David was too ill to attend the birthday party I had planned for the girls. He was rapidly approaching the end and it was his wish that his immediate family include me during this sad time. His family had always treated me well and they welcomed me as I attended his bedside as often as I could. This made it much easier on our sons than if the old hatred had remained in their father's heart. I drove to Dalton at least once a week to visit David and stand vigil with our sons. Jerry went with me when he wasn't working. At this point, I was taking three days a week away from my business and my husband to minister to my family's needs.

David died the last week of August. Jerry and I had a trip planned for that weekend. We were going to his daughter's house in Florida. They had moved out of state about a year after we married. I begged him to go without me, but he said that it was more important for him to be here with me.

After canceling our plans, we drove to Dalton. We arrived the night before the funeral. That evening, I received an urgent long distance call from Aunt Edris about my mother. She said my mother had become terribly confused. Aunt Edris was hysterical. She didn't know how to handle it. The only other person she could turn to was their brother-in-law who lived nearby. He came immediately, but he didn't know what to do either. Jerry and I had no choice but to leave immediately. I had to take care of matters at home. It was frustrating that I could *not* attend the funeral.

The healing continues

The next morning, I admitted my mother to the hospital. I immediately went to the graveside service for David. I could attend that service because they were burying him in a local cemetery. I had such conflicting emotions! My mother needed me. My sons needed me. I needed to bury David.

After the graveside service, I went back to the hospital. The news from the doctor was *not* good. He told me that my mother would no longer be able to live alone. He said that she would require nursing home care because of Alzheimer's disease.

The social services director at the hospital secured a room at a nursing home. It was too far from where I lived and I didn't think it would work out. However, Aunt Edris and I went to investigate the possibility of placing my mother in that facility. I was distressed to discover that she would be in a room with three others who were in the late stages of Alzheimer's. I believed that putting my mother there would be the same as a death sentence. Her quality of life would have diminished drastically. I didn't believe she would survive more than a few weeks.

Ultimately, I refused to put her in the nursing home. I wanted to see her often and I needed to be involved in her care. I didn't want a repeat of what my daddy had endured. I investigated personal care homes, but I realized she wouldn't be happy in one of those either. Besides, they were too expensive. We couldn't afford it.

I told the doctor I wanted to bring Mother home to live with me. I assured him I was prepared to tackle the job of taking care of her. He finally agreed that our home probably *would* be the best place for her.

Bringing my mother to live with us and selling her house meant that life would drastically change for all of us. Jerry had known from the beginning that I might eventually have the responsibility of caring for my parents and my aunt. Now, that difficult time had arrived. Jerry showed me what real love is all about as he welcomed Mother and Aunt Edris into our home and willingly shared me with them.

As the months passed, I assumed even more responsibility. I relied on my faith in God to help me through this difficult time in my life. As I practiced my faith, I began to understand why God's Word tells us not to marry outside our faith. I now had to work to prevent my desire for a religious home and Jerry's indifference from driving a wedge between us. I wanted to have a Christian home in every respect. However, I hadn't fully considered that when I made my choice to remarry. I don't regret for one minute having married Jerry. However, because we have no common spiritual bond, we have had to depend on *our love alone* to get us over the rough spots.

Past vs. present

I must constantly remember to recognize and acknowledge the line of demarcation between my pitiful past and my powerful present as I look forward to a promising future with eager anticipation.

Burdens

The ant is smart enough to use the piece of straw it is carrying as a bridge to cross a gap. Shouldn't we be intelligent enough to use our own burdens as stepping-stones to God?

The challenge of a lifetime

When Mother moved in with us, it meant that Aunt Edris would be alone. Coping with all the changes was difficult for Aunt Edris. She was afraid to be alone. We convinced her that moving in with us too, would be best for her. Although reluctant, she was too afraid of the alternatives to refuse. Fortunately, we had two rooms that we could fix up for them so that they would feel more at home.

In September, Mother came to live with us. In October, Aunt Edris came. We moved their furniture and personal effects into the two rooms I had emptied. Walking into each of their rooms was like going to their house to visit. They were delighted with the result.

Two days after my aunt moved, their brother-in-law, who had helped them in my absence, died suddenly. I was again in awe of God's incredible timing. Aunt Edris would have had no one to rely on for emergencies if she had not moved in with us when she did.

In November, on the anniversary of my daddy's death, Paul and his wife had a little girl! This beautiful little girl was a welcome relief for the sorrow and loss we had felt for so many months. With fair skin and blond hair, she was a little angel. Now, we had two granddaughters!

As the end of the year approached, I had to sell not only my mother's home, but my aunt's home as well. We had two houses on the market at the worst time of the year for real estate sales. Our real estate agent told us that if the houses didn't sell before Thanksgiving it could well be spring before a sale came through.

However, God has a wonderful way of making things work out! My aunt's house sold first. I had prayed it would because she was such a worrier. My mother's house sold the week my aunt's house closed. My mother's house closed in a record two weeks, just in time for Christmas.

In November, Jerry had cataract surgery and Aunt Edris was to have her first cataract surgery in December. Doctor visits seemed to be the thread that held the days together.

My granddaughter's birth had been the one bright spot in all of this. Watching this precious baby girl and seeing life go on in spite of everything encouraged all of us.

We scheduled my aunt to go for another cataract surgery in a month. The momentum slowed and, of course, I got sick. First one thing and then another plagued me for several months. The stress of twenty-four-hour nursing was beginning to affect me.

I was hoping that when Aunt Edris had her second surgery she would try to drive again, but she was too frightened to try. She gave up on life. She sat in front of her TV most of the time. Persuading her to go anywhere except out to eat once a week was difficult. She was obviously depressed. I had fought my own depression most of my life. Now I had to fight her depression as well.

Both Mother and Aunt Edris settled in quickly. Having the two of them here with us was wonderful. Mother liked to get out and go. However, she worried that something might happen to Aunt Edris while we were gone. Sometimes, to ease my mother's mind, Jerry would stay home with Aunt Edris so I could go out with my mother.

During the summer months, my business was extremely busy. My grandchildren came to visit. We had kids, sometimes one, sometimes two for about a month.

The challenge of a lifetime

In late August, Jerry and I took a three-day trip to the mountains and Mark came to granny-sit. I don't know what I would have done without him. He was always willing to take vacation days to let me have a break when I needed it!

While we were in the mountains, we went into a doll shop where I had seen collector dolls before. Beautiful dolls had always fascinated me. I never outgrew the desire to hold them. I saw one that was perfect. She was blonde, with blue eyes, and a precious face. I fell in love with her and we brought her home.

On our way back, I called home. Mother was confused again. She thought she had come to live with us only the day before. Every time I left for a day or so, or some traumatic event occurred, Mother would get worse. Somehow, with God's help, I always seemed able to say or do things that helped her to stay more in the present.

When we got home, I brought the new baby doll into Mother's room for her to see. Mother was like a little girl with a new toy. She immediately took the doll in her lap. She talked to the doll and crooned as if to a real infant. After about forty-five minutes of play my mother seemed totally focused and back in the real world.

I had wanted the doll for myself. However, I got more pleasure out of watching Mother hold it than I could have ever gotten by keeping it to myself. I gave her the doll to keep in her room.

When I mentioned my mother's interest in the doll to someone in the healthcare field, they told me that using baby dolls and pets with Alzheimer's patients is quite therapeutic.

I regret that Mother has had to go through this horrible nightmare and descent into madness. However, her inability to care for herself has allowed me to step in and take care of her. I have told her often that I consider it a privilege—not a burden to take care of her. These months have been the sweetest time I have ever spent with my mother. She seems to have forgotten that she didn't like me! And, I have rediscovered the depth of my love for her!

As caregiver to my childlike mother, I believe I understand the source of her pain. I have come to realize that any hurt she passed on to me was completely unintentional on her part. I'm so glad God gave me the grace to forgive her long before she got sick. It has freed me to go about the business of loving her and enjoying her company for the time left to us.

When I was twelve years old, I wrote a poem for her. A national church youth periodical published it. It described the mother-daughter relationship I wanted so badly then. God was good to allow us this time together. It has helped us both!

Mother, the sweetest one

Who is the dearest? Sweetest? Best?
The one who is always near,
The one who helped me stand life's test?
Mother, faithful and dear.

She's cared for me, toiled and striven,
Given her all for me,
To give me all I've ever been given:
I've a wonderful mother, see!

She always tucked me in at night
And heard me say my prayers,
Then she'd smile, turn out the light,
And leave me sleeping there.

I'm sure that when she has passed on
My heart will miss her so;
But in my heart she will remain
Wherever I may go!

That's 'cause she's been so very dear,
so kind to everyone,
And always very, very near…
Mother, The Sweetest One!

Laugh

Laugh more. Cry less. Quit complaining. People will welcome your company.

If only we could see the end from the beginning

The silence was broken as Mother quietly said, "You're tops in my book." She showed little emotion as she spoke. "I've never been one to pay compliments." She continued. "It has always been so hard for me to say I love you. I don't know why I am the way I am." She faltered as the emotion began to cloud her eyes with tears.

As I choked back my tears, I carefully took her arthritic hands in mine. I had waited fifty-six years to hear those words. The joy I felt at hearing them was quickly subdued because I felt her pain in that moment as surely as I had felt my own throughout the years.

I wish I could have taped that conversation so that I could hear it again. Instead, I will replay it in my head until it forms a permanent *tattoo* on my heart.

As I comforted Mother, she continued, "I have always felt so worthless, so inadequate. I was sure I didn't deserve love and I don't understand how you can be so good to me. You have your own life to live and you have given up so much to take care of Edris and me. I love you for it and appreciate it more than I can ever begin to tell you. Nevertheless, it just isn't fair to you. I'm so sorry you have to deal with all of this."

"Mother," I said, "I'm *not* doing this to be a martyr. I'm *not* doing this because someone thinks I should. I'm *not* doing this out of any sense of duty or obligation. I *am* doing this because I truly love you and want to take care of you. Even if Daddy hadn't asked me to take care of you, I would have!"

Although my feelings toward Mother have been genuine for a long time, today they seem especially so. She is gradually losing her ability to reason, rationalize and remember. As Alzheimer's ravages her mind, she has become less able to hide the emotional pain she has lived with all of her life. Now, with her barriers down, I am learning that perhaps we are *not* so different, after all.

My mother went on to confide in me the reasons that caused her to feel so inadequate. She said that she felt stigmatized by her pale blond hair, and was sure that everyone believed she bleached it. "In that era, only trashy women bleached their hair," she said. I thought, but did not say it, that if her eyesight hadn't been so bad, perhaps she would have realized that her blond roots told the truth. However, to coach her on how it could have been, if she had handled it differently, would serve only to make her feel more inadequate. My goal is to comfort her, not add to her pain. I pray daily that God will give me the wisdom to say and do the appropriate things to make this passage easier for my mother.

A few nights later, Mother used the phone to call me. At first, she was laughing because she thought it strange to call me on the phone when I was in the next room. Then she began to sob. "I need you," she said. "Please come in here and stay with me; I'm so afraid."

Reluctantly, I left Jerry to watch the movie alone as I went to comfort my mother. It was always hard to choose between tending her needs and spending time with him.

As I lay on the bed next to my mother, patting her arm, we talked about many things from the past and eventually got around to talking about the present. We talked about how sick I was recently. Shortly after recovering from flu and bronchitis, I had gallbladder surgery. While I was in the hospital, Aunt Edris suffered another heart attack and congestive heart failure. We all had to come to terms with the obvious. She would never get well.

If only we could see the end from the beginning

Mother was troubled that Aunt Edris was still in the hospital. We both missed her terribly.

My mother had already begun to grieve the imminent loss of her sister. She had lost another sister a few years before and the remaining siblings were in frail health. My Mother's physical health was quite good for her age, but this disease was slowly taking her away from us.

We talked for about thirty minutes as the sleeping pill she had taken earlier began to have an effect. I wanted to reassure her that I would be close by if she needed me for anything.

A time to grow up

I struck out on my own today;
It must have grieved your heart.
To love me so—yet see me go
And on life's journey start.

'Twas not an easy thing—to go,
And yet I could not stay.
Like those who've gone this way before
I, too, must go MY way.

There comes a time in all our lives
When we must do or die.
We have to spread our wings and try
To see if WE can fly.

Although YOU may have done it
And you know how far YOU got;
Until I've lived life for MYSELF
I won't know what is what.

The things you did—the way you lived
Has shaped YOU, don't you see.
Now it's my turn to live MY life
And shape me into ME.

So wish me well and bid me not
To forfeit life and stay
Forever in your shadow;
Let me live MY life today.

It's coming to an end.
Or, is this just the beginning?

My past was far behind me. I had difficulty realizing that I had actually lived through all the things about which I've written. The person I am now would never have lived that life. Yet, I realize that my strength comes because of where I have been and from what I endured.

Finally, it was making sense! My whole life had been about learning to lean on God and coming to understand His plan for my life. Each time I left the pathway He set before me, something pulled me back. He had presented alternate plans for me when my own stubborn, willful way didn't work out.

It took us completely by surprise when Cayce and his wife divorced that summer. I knew they had problems but none of us realized how bad it had gotten.

We lost our beloved ten-year-old Great Dane, Duchess, to kidney failure in mid-June. The loss affected us all profoundly. Even my mother, who had previously refused to touch any animal patted Duchess. Mother told Duchess that she loved her. Then we took Duchess on her last trip to the vet.

Jerry thought that we should get another Dane right away, but I wasn't so sure about that. There was never going to be another Duchess. I wasn't sure I could accept another dog into my heart just yet. Although I was reluctant, Jerry insisted. Sheba, a black Dane, joined our household and promptly won us over. Even our little Ty Ling, whom we got about a year after we married, loved her. Jerry was right. Having this new puppy did brighten things up for all of us.

In February 1997, Aunt Edris went into end-stage renal failure and started dialysis. At the time, she had a large open wound on her thigh. We had to dress the wound twice a day. She was in the hospital until mid-March. When she came home, we had a visiting nurse to help with her care. The wound finally healed in August. We enrolled Aunt Edris in Hospice and began to plan for the inevitable.

In spite of the doctor's prognosis, Aunt Edris got better and I began taking her on outings once a week. We went to the store to shop for clothes and to the movies. Oh, how she loved those special trips. Impulsively, I decided to take her on a trip to the mountains to see the fall colors. I knew how much she loved the mountains. I believe God gave me the impulse to go to the mountains right then just as surely as He had wakened me for my father's death.

I planned our trip for the first weekend in November. I picked Aunt Edris up after her dialysis treatment, and we headed to Maggie Valley, North Carolina. It was raining when we left, but magically the rain disappeared and the weather was beautiful for our trip. We spent the night there and went on to Cherokee, North Carolina the next day. On the way home, we drove through scenic Highlands. Aunt Edris said it was the most fun she had ever had on a trip. While on the way home, she reflected on how glad she was that she had come to live with me. She told me she appreciated that I had taught her how to live without being afraid. The time we shared that weekend was very special to me.

The following Tuesday she had surgery to replace the graft for the dialysis treatments. The first graft had closed. This was quite common so we weren't concerned. However, things didn't go so well and she suffered another heart attack a few hours after the surgery. The Hospice nurse administered a heavy-duty painkiller to make her more comfortable. It helped with the pain. However, Aunt Edris had run out of time. Her heart stopped beating Friday night just before midnight. God was merciful to allow her such a peaceful passing with me at her side.

Although I knew it was coming, I was ill prepared for how my aunt's death devastated me. She had always been like a big sister to me. When she came to live with us, she became my best friend. As I took care of her over those last few months, she became my child. In many ways, she had been a mother to me as well. I felt as if my heart could stand no more!

Although I had been handling her affairs for several years, I now had to handle her estate as well. It was a difficult task, yet one that helped me fulfill promises I made to her and helped me cope with my loss.

Naturally, the death of Aunt Edris left Mother in worse shape. She became more confused than ever. I realized the day was approaching when she would forget that I was her daughter. Thinking about losing my mother was painful. She was almost eighty but her physical health was stable. Jerry was only a year younger. I thought of how lonely it will be for me when they are both gone from my life.

I realized that the level of care that Mother would probably need over the coming months would increase. I wondered if I was up to the task of running a business and caring for her simultaneously.

I had faced many difficulties since starting the business. However, God had provided the workflow so that when I needed time for my family, business would diminish. When I needed the work to pay the bills, it would always miraculously appear. During the months when I needed to spend most of my time caring for my aunt, less work came in. Shortly after she died, the workflow picked up again. When I looked back on it all, I realized that God had been in control all along. I knew in my heart that He did *not* bring me this far just to let me down!

God's pathway

God used my trail of broken hearts and failed relationships to lead me into the fullness of His grace.

God blessed me with furry friends

I got my first kitten several months after my aunt died. About eight months later, I got another. A year later four more kittens joined our family.

Our household now consists of six cats, two dogs and two humans. There is never a dull moment. The unique personalities of each have blended into the fabric of a very special family.

Ty Ling, the miniature Shih Tzu we had gotten about a year after we married was the boss. When we first got him, he weighed less than a pound. From his attitude, you would have thought he was the Dane! From the beginning, he had no trouble intimidating Duchess. She treated him like her baby. She spoiled him and let him get away with anything, but Sheba was a challenge. Big, black, clumsy and full of love, Sheba doted on the kitties. She lovingly put Ty Ling in his place by holding him down with a big paw. Sheba loved to spend her evenings at our feet as we watched TV. She wanted to be a lap dog, but she quickly grew too big for that.

Although our six cats were from five different litters, we pulled together a family of animals that interacted in a loving way. All of the cats were rescued animals.

When I went to the vet to get a kitten for my granddaughter, I chose Sassy, a tortoise calico. However, while waiting for the vet to check her over, we bonded and I couldn't part with her. She is the mouthpiece for the group when they want treats. She comes and pats my arm much like a child trying to get Mama's attention.

Sonny Boy, now a fifteen-pound red and white tabby, joined our family about eight months later. He is quite shy around strangers, and is a real "Mama's boy." He worries if I change my routine, and if I'm not feeling well he hovers over me. If I leave anything out of place or fail to follow a routine, he "talks" to me and tells me about it. He entices me to follow him through the house looking at everything to be sure things are in order.

The identical twins, my black beauties, came next. I couldn't decide which one to adopt. Jerry said we shouldn't separate them, so we adopted both. Siara is the friendlier of the two and quite vocal. She loves my home office. She sits in my lap while I work. Sabrina is extremely shy, almost never speaks, and is in love with Sonny.

Scarlet, a beautiful, longhaired red and white bundle of energy has never met a stranger. She leaps into laps, purrs and welcomes everyone with a kiss. She is an escape artist who loves to play "beat it out the door" while we fall all over ourselves trying to stop her.

Samantha, another tortoise calico, was destined to be mine. With Samantha's adoption, I knew our family would be complete. I had chosen her name and I knew what she would look like before I met her. I went from one rescue group to another looking for her. I knew immediately when I saw her that she was *my* Samantha. She obviously knew too, for when I said, "Is your name Samantha?" she jumped from the cage into my arms and refused to turn me loose. When I got her home, she let the rest of the group know that I was now *her* "mommy" and she was *not* interested in sharing.

I worried that Sassy would have her feelings hurt, but she was very gracious. She stepped back and let Samantha have her way until she was a year old. Then one day, Sassy stepped into my lap, looked at Samantha as if to say, "Okay, kiddo, you're *not* a baby anymore. Let's share." Samantha moved over and they have shared my lap ever since, taking turns or cuddling together in my arms. At night, Sassy loves to sleep in the crook of my arm. Samantha sleeps next to my pillow.

When Sheba was five years old, she injured her back and could hardly get onto her feet. The thought that it might be serious was devastating. Although it had been a good while since our other losses, considering the possibility of another loss was difficult. We were afraid the vet was going to have to put her to sleep. I talked to the other "family members." I explained that their "big sister" was very sick and needed comfort. It was amazing to watch as they gathered around and took turns going over to Sheba to kiss and comfort her before we took her to the vet. Sheba subsequently recovered after several weeks. Each cat *and* Ty Ling continued to bestow special affection on Sheba throughout her ordeal.

This touching incident firmly convinced me that our blended family did *not* happen by chance but by design. I believe that God, in His infinite wisdom and mercy, sent each of these precious pets to me to help in my journey to emotional health.

I can't begin to tell you how much comfort these dear animals have been to me over the last few years. They have filled a void in my life and given me the affection and companionship I needed after I gave up my role as family caregiver. Besides, who else would have sat on my manuscript all these months as I tried to finish the edits?

Surprises

Life is full of surprises. If you don't believe it, just say the word never.

In closing

Many other significant events have transpired in my life. My heart is full of tattoos. However, in this journal, I have only mentioned those that have had the greatest impact on my life. I hope that, having read my story, you will become inspired to overcome whatever it is in your life that may have caused you to despair. I hope that my book will help you to recognize the positive tattoos of your own life and collect them as treasures. I pray that painful tattoos of your heart will be rare, and never self-inflicted. I pray that you have gained from this book the strength to rise above it all. I pray that you will seek to renew and restore broken relationships. If this book has helped or inspired you, then it will have been worth my painful recital.

Remember this: a smart person learns from his or her mistakes. A truly wise person learns from the mistakes of others! *Be wise!*

You've heard it said, "Be careful of what you say. You may have to eat your words." I would like to expand on that theme. Be careful what you choose. Every choice you make has a resulting consequence. Be very sure you are willing to live with the consequences of your choices! *Most important of all, be sure you are willing for those you love most to live with them as well!*

In the pages that follow, you will read letters from my sons. They wrote to me expressing the thoughts this book provoked for each of them after reading the *first draft*. They have *not* yet read the final copy. Stephen and Cayce were the first to respond. Their letters brought me a great deal of peace and brought us even closer.

I fully expected an angry letter from Mark because he had suffered so much, but Paul's letter took me by surprise. Somehow, I had failed to convey to him that I **do** take full responsibility for my choices.

The point I had wished to make with this book was that, *through my acceptance of responsibility* and allowing God to work in my life, I had changed.

Reading their letters deeply saddened me. The pain and anger they felt and expressed was almost palpable. I chose to include all four letters in this book although two are painful to read. I believe these letters *may be the most important part* of this book because they show the impact my poor choices had on *all* of my sons.

The prayer/song following this chapter is one that I wrote. It became a bridge across the painful separation between my parents and me. It helped tremendously to rebuild our relationship.

A sinner's prayer

Dear Lord, It's been a long, long time
Since I knelt down to pray.
And—Lord, it's—well—it's just so hard
To find the words to say.
I'd like to have a talk with you Dear Jesus—if I may.
Please—Jesus—come and help me now…
To find the words to say…

When I was just a little child, my mother said to me
That I should leave the world behind and follow after Thee.
But, as the years passed on and I neglected her advice,
My life was ruined—My spirit broke; and now I've paid the price.

Lord, grant me now, I humbly pray forgiveness for my sins.
My soul is lost, my future gone, if you are not my friend.
Restore in me the Christian traits my parents sought to teach.
Receive this wandering soul of mine, and mend this lonely breach.

Too long I've walked this worldly path and now sin's scars I bear.
My mother cried, my father prayed; too little did I care.
Now with Your help, I'll try to do the very best I can.
God—bless them now—I love them so; and help them understand.

Lord, grant me now, I humbly pray the grace to make amends
For all the pain I've surely caused; the heartaches without end.
Reclaim my soul and set me free so I may live again.
And gently guide me in Your Way and always hold my hand.

I want my parents now to know their prayers were not in vain.
I've turned around and changed my course and I am not the same.
I'm sure they'll have a rich reward, 'cause they took time to care.
You know that it's because of them I've prayed this earnest prayer.

Tattoos of the Heart

> Lord, grant me now, I humbly pray the strength to carry on.
> My heart is low, my head is bowed; it's hard to walk alone.
> Shine on my path and show the way that You would have me take.
> Walk with me Lord, and make of me a blessing for Thy sake.
>
> Amen

2003 update

My mother continues her descent into oblivion because of Alzheimer's disease. However, there is hope for the future because of a pending inheritance from her cousin's estate. When that comes through, I can bring her home if there is enough money to hire part time help to care for her. I pray that the money will be sufficient and that it will come before it is too late for her to benefit from it.

Mark and his family have bought a new home and moved to the country. Their son is now a budding artist.

Paul suffered two strokes that left him permanently disabled. When his health began to fail, he sold his custom framing business. As a stay-at-home dad, he is the kind of parent I wish my boys had known. He has taken up sewing and quilting. As with everything else he has tried, he is quite good at it.

Stephen and his wife reconciled their marriage after a short separation. He is continuing his career as a baker and recently started a specialized baking business on a part-time basis. He and his wife foster rescued cats and kittens.

A job-related injury permanently disabled Cayce. He has since married a lovely young woman with three children. Cayce's attempt to gain full custody of his children was unsuccessful. The children were suffering emotionally and he believed the best thing he could do for everyone was to give up custody. Their stepfather subsequently adopted them. To my eternal regret, Cayce now understands, from both perspectives, much of what I experienced.

Jerry and I are approaching our eleventh anniversary. We go to ballroom dances with our friends two or three times a week. The bandleaders usually invite me to sing with them as a guest vocalist. Life is good! I enjoy every day to the fullest as I wait to see what God has planned for my future.

And…life goes on, as I watch while my children accumulate their own heart's tattoos.

Author's note

In the telling of my story, I have attempted to be honest and sincere. I do *not* solicit your sympathy. Self-pity is *not* something in which I choose to indulge. I have grieved my way through loss of innocence and the indelible *tattoos* my decisions have left on my heart and psyche and moved on.

I must stress that this is merely a recital of the events that have resulted in "tattoos" on *my* heart. It is not an attempt to blame anyone or any event for the choices that *I* made. When I became an adult, I could have chosen to change my direction at any time. Sadly, I did not exercise this option until I was almost forty years old.

I do *not* want to hurt anyone by telling of these events. I do *not* want to hurt my sons. They were innocent children who had no alternative but to participate in the three-ring circus that my choices in life created for them.

I especially do *not* wish to hurt or embarrass my parents. Although they may have helped to set the stage for my mis-choices in life, *I take full responsibility* for those choices. My parents did the best they could with the knowledge they possessed. They were products of their own upbringing. In addition, they had no idea what emotional damage was or how it would ultimately affect their child as an adult.

I do *not* want to hurt any of the men I chose to marry! We hurt each other enough during our relationships. To spare everyone involved hurt and embarrassment, I chose to use fictitious names when I first began to realize this journal would become a book. After my second son read the finished manuscript, he said he would prefer that I use his real name. He said it was too hard to remember who was who otherwise. When I asked my other sons, they also felt comfortable with having their names used. However, in the final edits, I decided to change or leave out the names of my daughters-in-law and my grandchildren to spare them any potential embarrassment.

From Mark, a.k.a. David the Poet 2/14/99

Dear Mother,

Your book about our family really didn't have an impact on my life but rather resurrected some very painful memories that will always have an effect on my life simply because they are part of the sum total of who I am and will become in the future.

It was the events themselves that have had and continue to have the greatest impact on my life; events that I have never been able to fully escape or overcome. Because, in order to leave them behind it would mean I'd have to leave each and everyone of the members of my family behind as I blaze my own path without looking back.

The one thing that put your many marriages in perspective for me was the statement you made about having grown up with a mother who controlled her relationship with her husband, your father. You grew up with the idea that it was a woman's right to control her relationship with her husband and family.

This idea, I believe, is what ultimately led you to divorce my father when you lost your bid to control him and what caused you to fail in so many other relationships until you decided to stick it out with Pops (Paul) until he passed away.

The upheavals, as a child, youth and young adult, that I was forced to endure like a never-ending roller coaster along with the cloud of depression that I still battle, has left me bereft of the stability that everyone needs as the cornerstone of their life.

The consequences of the physical and emotional abuse I suffered at the hands of my stepmother and a couple of my stepfathers along with the unending war of the women's movement against men has completely shattered the trust that I need to be able to have a meaningful relationship with my wife.

Tattoos of the Heart

In the end, all that can be said of the emotional legacy you and my father have left for me to carry on with is "With the current generation of women raised by your generation, it can be truly asked: 'Who needs enemies?'"

Sincerely,
Mark a.k.a. David, the Poet

From Paul, February 15, 1999

Mom,

I am writing this letter in the 11th hour, not because I am the world's worst procrastinator, but because after reading your book, Tattoos of the Heart, I was left with so many conflicting thoughts and emotions that even now I find it very difficult to put those thoughts on paper.

Reading from your perspective has given me insight into the way you see things, how you cope with what has happened to you in your early life, and later with the things you caused to happen both to yourself and to those around you.

Throughout your book I got the impression of, 'poor pitiful me. See what the world has made me do,' followed by a kind of acceptance of responsibility for your own actions, then back to 'it's not all my fault, look at all the negatives in my childhood…all the way back to the womb.'

I'm sorry. I don't buy that theory. Look at MY childhood! If you apply your logic to my life, I shouldn't have been able to find someone who loves me, build a successful career, have a stable marriage, father two of the world's most wonderful children, and live my version of the American dream. But, I have…and then some!

Sure, my life hasn't been all sunshine and roses. I have had my troubles and failures too. I think that the biggest difference between us is that at a very early age I realized that I am the one who is responsible for what I do, what I will become, and whether I am happy or not. I made a conscious decision about what I was going to do, or not do, with my life. I think at some point everyone does. Once that choice is made, whatever happened before no longer counts.

Mom, you have come a long way. You have progressively made better decisions for several years and they have led you to the happiness and security you were looking for all of your life. I only wish you had started sooner. Keep it up.

I love you because you are my mother and you gave me life. I haven't always liked the things you have done, but I will always love you.

Your Son,
Paul

From Stephen, April 25, 1998

Dear Mom,

Thank you! Your book was the greatest gift you have ever given me! It has validated our lives, my life, especially! I have never read any book as fast as I did this one. In spite of working two jobs, I made time to finish it. Reading it was both painful and enjoyable. It was as if I were living my life all over again. However, this time the missing pieces were there; I could see the whole picture, not just my child's perspective. As I read, I gained a better understanding of who you were then and who you are now. Understanding you helps me to understand myself as well.

As you know, I have been in and out of counseling with many different therapists. Some helped more than others and some not at all. I believe that if I had read your book several years ago, I would have needed less counseling and would have benefited more from any I did get. I also think it would have made a big difference in my marriage. If I ever feel the need for more counseling, I will have the book in my hand when I go. It will make the process much easier if I share this book with the therapist.

Shortly after my wife left me, I lost my second job. During the free time I had then, I began to examine my life to see what had gone so wrong. After much prayer and meditation, I decided to get my life back on track. I turned myself over to God and gave up smoking and drinking. I even gave up 18 cups of coffee every day! I was over the withdrawal by the time you came to visit, and your visit was very timely. Actually, Mom, it was the first time I had wanted you to visit me on my own turf. I know from what you said that it was the first time you had truly wanted to be there as well. Our relationship had been very awkward since that day in the courtroom when it seemed that you had abandoned me! Thanks to the letter you wrote to us when dad died, you and I have picked up the pieces and with this book, the healing is complete.

Mom, I really think you should try to publish this book using your real name and I am comfortable with you using my real first name as well. It makes it even more valid if you don't try to disguise our identities. Your book is a testimony to how your consequences became ours as well, and how you rose above it all. Being honest about your identity can potentially help others when you have the opportunity to share this story with them.

I hope that many will read and profit from your book. It has something valuable for anyone from a broken home or for someone who is considering breaking up his or her home. It can help them see that all they are and all they do will ultimately affect their children. Hopefully they will think twice before making such drastic moves.

Finally, Mom, I love you and I'm very proud of you, and proud to be your son.

Love always,
Stephen

Thoughts from Cayce—May 11, 1998

My mother handed me this book. She said, "Here, I want you to read this and tell me what you think."

I had no idea this book was going to help me work through so many different emotions—emotions I had chosen to bury deep inside. I hadn't realized there were still some areas in my life that required closure.

Growing up we learn many things from our parents. I wish I could say, "They taught me everything I needed to know and I've learned from their mistakes; and I haven't made the same mistakes." But, those would not be accurate statements. I have made some of the same choices/mistakes, and, sometimes I made different choices/mistakes when faced with life's challenges.

As I read this book, I began to understand certain things about my Mother. Even though I returned at the age of ten and lived with her until I became an adult, I rarely had any idea what was really happening to her. I was too busy—being a mischievous little kid—then I was too busy trying to be an adult.

Through reading this book, I relived many events—some happy, some sad, and some tragic.

I want to thank my Mother for sharing this book with me (and with you, too). I have benefited from it in many ways. I only hope you can benefit from it as well.

One last thing I have learned: It is true. "Life is a cycle." But, "History repeats itself"—only if we choose to let it.

Leave!

However difficult it may be, leave your pitiful circumstances! But, don't leave bitter! Leave better!

Statistics

David and I were married nine years. We have three sons: Mark (a.k.a. David, the Poet), Paul and Stephen.

Kenn and I were married four years. We have one son, Kenneth (also known as Cayce).

Tony and I were married twice for a total of a year-and-a-half.

Sam and I were married six months.

Marco and I were married two years.

Paul and I had been married almost eight years when he died.

Jerry and I were married in 1992 and are still like newlyweds!

My relationships with my daughters-in-law and grandchildren are good. However, since *they* did not live through the major events in this story, they do not have a prominent place in this book. Consequently, to protect their privacy, I have intentionally omitted their names.

0-595-74562-8